Capital Structure, Managerial Incentives
and Corporate Governance

AF793652

Widmung und Dank

Diese Dissertation ist während meiner Zeit als wissenschaftlicher Mitarbeiter am Lehrstuhl für Wirtschaftstheorie von Professor Dr. Jürgen Eichberger an der Universität des Saarlandes entstanden. Ich bin Teilnehmern des Forschungsprivatissimums an der Universität des Saarlandes zu großem Dank verpflichtet, die meine Forschung mit ihren Anregungen und ihrer Kritik unterstützt haben. Des weiteren danke ich Seminarteilnehmern an folgenden Universitäten, an denen ich Teile der Arbeit zur Diskussion stellen konnte: Australian National University (Canberra), Universität Bern (Tagung des Vereins für Socialpolitik, 1997), Universität Dortmund, Humboldt Universität Berlin (Workshop on Corporate Governance, 1998), Université Lumière, Lyon II, University of Melbourne, Monash University (Melbourne) und Universität Toulouse (Econometric Society Meeting, 1997).

Ulrich Bindseil, Guido Gehendges, Justus Haucap, Roman Inderst, Joachim Keller, Roland Kirstein, Stefan Preiß, Peter Strobel und Jens Tapking haben mir in unzähligen Diskussionen mit ihren Anregungen geholfen. Die Arbeit hat erheblich davon profitiert, daß ich in den Jahren 1993 bis 1996 an den von Professor Dr. Dr. h.c. Rudolf Richter bzw. von Professor Dr. Urs Schweizer organisierten Sommerschulen zu Vertragstheorie teilnehmen durfte. Insbesondere die Sommerschule zur Vertragstheorie mit Patrick Bolton und Mathias Dewatripont (August 1996 in Oberwesel) hat mir wertvolle Anregungen geliefert.

Jürgen Eichberger und Christian Keuschnigg haben die Arbeit mit großem Interesse verfolgt und mich durch ihre Kommentare auf Beweislücken und begriffliche Defizite aufmerksam gemacht. Zu besonderem Dank bin ich Jürgen Eichberger verpflichtet, der mein Verständnis für Vertragstheorie und Kapitalstruktur erheblich geprägt hat.

Für finanzielle Unterstützung danke ich der Universität des Saarlandes, der Universität Melbourne, der BMW AG und dem Verein für Socialpolitik.

Schließlich danke ich meiner Frau Marion, Annette Pfeil und besonders meinen Eltern für ihre Unterstützung während der Fertigstellung der Arbeit. Ihnen sei sie gewidmet.

Saarlouis im Oktober 2001 C.M.P.

TABLE OF CONTENTS

Chapter 1

Introduction

1.1 The Capital Structure Problem

Few topics in economic theory have received as much attention as the theory of capital structure. The question how firms finance their investment and what determines their choice has occupied the academic profession for several decades. Economic theory has developed a large number of models that identify various determinants of the firm's financing decision, among them bankruptcy, taxes and informational issues. Bankruptcy and tax considerations are certainly of great empirical relevance to the question, yet firms exhibit similar patterns of financing behavior across countries with very different bankruptcy laws and fundamentally different tax provisions. This suggests that there are other forces at work, which impact the firm's financing decision beyond those country specific aspects. It is widely accepted today that these forces must be related to the structure of the informational environment in which the firm is operating. Therefore, informational economics has become the most common and most successful approach to explain the observed financing behavior of firms. A brief historical sketch of the theoretical debate will help to understand better today's state of the art in research on capital structure theory.

Contributions to the theory of capital structure fall into three different periods which are divided by two crucial events. The first one is marked by the publication of an article by Modigliani and Miller in 1958 which has heavily influenced almost all research done on this topic since then. The second event can be seen in the development of the economics of information and its application to the corporate finance literature in the early 1970s.

In the pre-Modigliani-Miller era it was generally held that the value of the firm could be maximized by a diligent choice of capital structure, i.e. the relation of debt to equity financing.[1] Modigliani and Miller [1958] opposed this reasoning on grounds of an arbitrage argument which roughly runs as follows. A rational investor is aware that debt has the potential to boost the firm's valuation. If capital markets are perfect, any investor can borrow on the same terms as the firm and therefore an individual investor is able to replicate any advantage of debt financing on his own. Arbitrage will then eliminate the advantages of debt financing and some given capital structure will be as good as any other. According to this view, different mixtures of debt and equity are simply alternatives to allocate claims to the firm's cash flow, but the value of the firm remains unaffected by the different choices. This result was heavily debated immediately after its publication in 1958 and opponents mainly criticized the model'' underlying assumptions in order to re-establish the relevance of capital structure for the valuation of the firm.

Stiglitz [1969] has become the standard reference for the Modigliani-Miller results, but by now the theory can also be found in any textbook on corporate finance or financial economics.[2] He embeds the Modigliani-Miller argument into a general equilibrium framework which hinges heavily on two prerequisites. First of all, bankruptcy is excluded and secondly, individual investors must have access to the same terms of debt financing as firms. Both assumptions are fairly restrictive. This makes the theory vulnerable against opposition, since giving up any one or both of the assumptions will invalidate the theorem.[3] A new theory emanated from this state of research in the early 1970s. Kraus and Litzenberger [1973] developed a model which explains the firm's financing decision as a trade-off between the tax benefits of debt against the expected cost of bankruptcy associated with debt financing.

Eventually, the development of the economics of information provided new analytic tools which completely altered the nature of arguments from the early

[1] For an exposition of this traditional view see for example Brealey and Myers [1991, pp. 407] or Copeland and Weston [1988, pp. 444].

[2] The following textbooks contain detailed presentations of the Modigliani-Miller theorem: Brealey and Myers [1991, pp. 398], Copeland and Weston [1988, pp. 437] and Eichberger and Harper [1997, pp. 158].

[3] See Eichberger and Harper [1997, pp. 162] for remarks on that issue.

1970s on. Until then, contributions had merely questioned the assumptions on which the Modigliani-Miller result was built upon. Now, financial economics turned to informational aspects which were not even mentioned in previous formulations of the irrelevance result. The informational approach is dominating the theory of capital structure since then and it will also serve as a basis for this book which aims at studying issues related to the financing of the firm's operation and investment.

The economics of information analyzes informational frictions among economic agents and institutions as they arise in the course of economic activity. One can hardly imagine how corporate finance literature could do without this paradigm, since informational frictions are ubiquitous to the financing decision. Some investors may have better information on a firm's earning prospects than others, a financier may not be able to observe the diligence of the firm's management and a bank may have difficulties to distinguish good from bad debtors. A neoclassical framework is not suited to address any of those issues, because it fails to spell out the information structure among agents and institutions. Traditional neoclassical theory is rather viewing the firm as a black box, without paying any attention to how the production process is actually taking place.

Before economic theorists start to analyze the firm's financing behavior with the newly developed instruments, corporate finance is neoclassical in the sense that the firm's cash flow is assumed to be exogenously given. No effort is made whatsoever to explain where this cash flow originates from and what factors influence its determination. This fundamentally changes through the application of information economics. Now, the cash flow is no longer exogenously specified, but affected by the informational friction that is prevailing. By influencing this underlying friction, capital structure has an impact on the expected cash flow and thereby regains its relevance for the firm's valuation. But even though the application of informational economics to the theory of capital structure has been very successful, this approach seems to have deficiencies, some of which shall be addressed in this book.

Firstly, many informational frictions are too lightly transferred to the corporate finance context, that is, theoretical models often employ capital structure to perform a task for which equivalent tools exist. Quite frequently, this is done without justifying any further why capital structure is brought in. Especially models which postulate a role for capital structure in alleviating conflicts of interest suffer from this flaw. It is often questionable why a firm should manipulate its capital structure to influence such a friction in its favor, if there are more obvious tools available to achieve this. Chapter 2 of this book aims at proposing a theoretical foundation for employing capital structure as a tool to mitigate the adverse effect of this informational problem in addition to the more obvious tool of monetary compensation.

Secondly, most informational approaches consider the firm's financial choice in isolation without reference to financial markets and institutions. This is short-sighted, since one should expect that the functioning of markets and the financial services provided through institutions as banks can make a significant contribution to explaining financial behavior. Banks are sometimes attributed a role in disciplining firm management within countries where close firm-bank relationships are existing. This type of argument is often made in a non-technical manner by describing the empirical evidence in countries like Japan and Germany whose financial systems show such institutional arrangements. Chapter 3 tries to embed the argument into a formal framework which may help to clarify the role which banks are playing for a company's decision to finance its investment.

Thirdly, some theories are heavily challenged by empirical studies to the point that theory cannot maintain its original position anymore. This is especially true for the branch of literature which falls back on ideas from industrial organization. To some extent this is the case since the theoretical predictions of those theories are quite accessible for empirical testing as compared to other lines of research in capital structure theory. Chapter 4 will introduce a model, in which the underlying friction is a problem of asymmetric information. That Chapter will direct attention to a recent empirical challenge of theoretical approaches which seek to explain a link between financial markets and product markets. The aim of the Chapter is to propose a theory within the industrial organization approach which can be reconciled with empirical evidence.

The different types of informational frictions and the special problems that accompany them constitute a natural pattern for distinguishing the different branches of the financing literature and alloting theoretical contributions to different categories. The remainder of this Chapter is structured as follows: Before we review some representative examples of the existing literature, we will first take a closer look at the differences of debt and equity, which constitute the basis for any theory of capital structure. Section 3 will then present a selection of theories upon which our own contributions in Chapters 2 to 4 are built. A large part of this book views capital structure as a governance device, i.e. a tool that helps investors to safeguard or to increase returns on their investment. Section 4 will therefore put financing into the larger perspective of governance mechanisms. Finally, Section 5 will give a brief description of the three models in the following Chapters.

1.2 Features of Debt and Equity

In a sense, informational theories of capital structure have two ingredients. Each theory combines a problem from informational economics with a certain view on debt and equity and thus emphasizes different aspects and different properties of the two financial instruments. In order to see the common elements of the existing informational approaches with respect to the view on debt and equity they take, we will now collect and explain the most important differences between the two securities.

A first part of this Section will describe the differences between debt and equity as they concern the claims on the cash flow to which a holder of such a security is entitled and make some remarks on securityholders' rights to influence the firm's decision process. This will be followed by comments on the issue of bankruptcy with its special consequences for management.

1.2.1 Payout Structure and Voting Rights

Very generally speaking, debt and equity are simply different types of claims to the firm's cash flow. Debt is a claim of a fixed size, while equity shows a variable payout structure, since it returns a variable dividend depending on profits to its holders, if any. Equityholders make the firm's operating decision as long as the firm can service its debt obligations, while creditors do not directly influence the firm's operating decisions. Debtholders are compensated for this concession in the sense that their claims are senior to those of equityholders, i.e. creditors must be paid up before equityholders obtain any receipts. Given a stochastic cash flow, the firm may be unable to repay a fixed amount of money to its creditors. If the firm fails to do so, it is said to be bankrupt. Upon bankruptcy, control shifts to creditors, who then have the right to recover their outstanding claims and to command how to proceed with the distressed firm.[4]

In spite of many years of research the basic payout structure of debt and equity is not well understood. Why are some claims to the firm's cash flow fixed, while others receive what's left over? After all, both are just supplying funds for investment. Gale and Hellwig [1985] present a model that gives a theoretical foundation for debt's specific payout scheme. Since it is so fundamental to the theory of finance, we will sketch their model here.

A creditor supplies funds to an investor, who finances an investment project with random return. Both share beliefs over realizations of the cash flow, but upon realization, there prevails an asymmetry of information between both sides. While the investor directly observes the realization, the creditor can only do so at some (monitoring) cost. In the absence of monitoring, this leads to a misrepresentation problem, since the investor may claim insufficient funds to repay a promised amount if he can lower his repayment load that way.

---

[4] Often, a bankrupt firm is worth more as a going concern as compared to the amount which could be recovered by selling the firm piecemeal. It is then reasonable to reorganize the firm rather than to liquidate it. The laws which organize the processes of liquidation and reorganization differ from country to country. In the United States, for example, Chapter 11 of the Bankruptcy Code provides rules for such a reorganization. Chapter 7 of the same law governs the liquidation process under which the firm's assets are sold to cover the creditors claims.

The standard debt contract is (under certain conditions) the product of a contract design problem, which economizes on these monitoring costs. Saving on such cost is in the best interest of both parties, since the receipts left over after accounting for monitoring cost are available for distribution between the two. An incentive compatible contract must elicit truthtelling by the investor, i.e. he must only claim insufficient funds if this is indeed the case. It is due to this incentive compatibility that loan repayment is constant for states in which the investor does not declare bankruptcy. If repayment were to increase with reported receipts, there would be an incentive to understate. With a fixed repayment in non-bankrupt states, the investor will never be tempted to lie about the generated cash flow and monitoring can be avoided for those states. The creditor can therefore restrict verification of receipts to those cases in which the investor claims insufficiency of funds to repay.[5]

The informational situation of stockholders in large corporations is not very different from the informational asymmetry described by Gale and Hellwig. It is thus not entirely clear why some parties are paid off on a fixed basis, while others can claim the rest. The security design literature, which endogenizes financial contracts and addresses issues of optimal payout structure and voting rights has contributed more to our understanding of specific security forms (see Harris and Raviv [1989, 1995] and Zender [1991]). We will rather take the somewhat more traditional view in this book and assume that the payout structures and attached voting rights are exogenously given.

The payout structure of debt is an important element for those informational theories of capital structure which postulate a role of financing in alleviating diverging interests between fund providers and the management of the firm. If the firm management is inclined to reinvest earnings in negative net-present-value projects, shareholders will rather prefer to force management to disgorge these funds. Debt with its fixed payout can be such a device, since it withdraws funds from the management, which might otherwise be invested to the

[5] Eichberger and Harper [1997, pp. 182] present Gale's and Hellwig's argument in a more elegant way than the original paper and we refer to this reference for a more in depth analysis.

disadvantage of shareholders. But this role of debt is rather vague, because dividends could also be fixed at a certain level to obtain the same effect.[6] The argument however goes that debt is a "hard claim" in contrast to dividend payments which are under the discretion of those who run the firm on behalf of shareholders.

Apart from differences in the payout structure, the control issue seems to be a further basic characteristic of the two financial instruments. the issue of control manifests itself in the voting rights that are sometimes attached to equity. Equityholders are in charge of the firm's business decision as long as bankruptcy can be avoided. Unlike debtholders, they are considered as owners of the firm. Ownership can be concentrated as in the case, where a family is the sole owner of a firm, but it can also be dispersed over a large number of stockholders as in the case of a large publicly trades corporation. Voting rights permit stockholders to participate in the selection of the board of directors and other special issues and thus enable them to influence the firm'' decision making at least via the choice of representatives who run the firm on their behalf. Voting rights are playing an eminent role for the financing decision, if a party (e.g. the management or an owner-entrepreneur) must fear to lose control over the firm through a dilution of control rights.

Equity capital can take on various forms. For example, the private funds of an entrepreneur invested in her firm are equity. So are stock and retained earnings, i.e. returns which have not been paid out to stockholders as dividends. Stock in turn may come in many disguises. There are types of stock which rather resemble debt in the fact that this stock does not give any voice to its holders in firm decisionmaking. Preferred stock, for example, is senior to common stock, but has (in general) no voting rights attached. Common stock in contrast entitles

[6] We will return to this point when we review the existing theoretical literature on that issue.

its holders to one vote in the election of directors.[7] Speaking of stock, we will always have in mind common stock with one vote per share.[8]

As in the case of equity, there is a large variety of debt. Debt can be the claim of a financial institution (such as a commercial bank or a savings bank) against the firm's cash flow, or many individuals may be the creditors if claims are publicly traded. Additionally, debt can differ in the riskiness of the claim, the term structure etc.[9]

1.2.2 Bankruptcy and Reputation

As we have seen, the two financial instruments of debt and equity are different in very obvious dimensions, like the voting rights attached to them or the payout they promise. One more indirect distinguishing feature is that debt financing creates the risk of bankruptcy, while equity capital does not. Parties involved into the firm's business may incur cost, if the firm is unable to service its debt obligation. The most obvious cost are those incurred by the firm, when it undergoes financial distress. These cost are mainly attributed to administrative aspects of bankruptcy, the disruption of business, organizational matters of liquidation or restructuring and so forth. Since the trade-off between tax advantages of debt and bankruptcy cost was long held as a major determinant for the firm's choice of capital structure, the measuring of those cost has been the subject of several empirical investigations (e.g. see Altman [1984]; Ang, Chua and McConnell [1982], Bradley, Jarrell and Kim [1984] and Warner [1977]).

Bankruptcy cost accruing to the firm's management are another type of cost, which is of special interest to us here, since these cost constitute an important element of several informational theories of capital structure. There are many

---

[7] We cannot go into detail with respect to the different types of stock and we refer to Chapter 15 of Copeland and Weston [1992] plus the references therein for those issues.

[8] Grossman and Hart [1988] and Harris and Raviv [1988] each present a model in which this socalled one share/one vote structure is part of the socially optimal mechanism for allocating control among management teams with different abilities to run the firm.

[9] It is outside the scope of this book to give a detailed survey on those issues and we refer the interested reader to Chapter 24 of Copeland and Weston [1992].

reasons why bankruptcy can be unattractive to the management. Bankruptcy might be interpreted as a sign of incompetence by the managerial labor market and therefore managers' human capital may suffer. Fama argues along these lines when he says that "the rental rates for [managers'] human capital signaled by the managerial labor market are likely to depend on success or failure of the firm" (Fama [1980, 291-2]).[10]

Gilson [1989] presents a detailed study for these cost to management. He investigates the effects of financial distress on managers' career paths and finds that approximately 71% of senior managers in his sample have been expelled from office two years after their firm filed for bankruptcy. The data seem to suggest that bankruptcy is indeed perceived as something that casts doubt on managers' skill, since none of them holds a comparable position in another company three years after financial distress. This also suggests that salaries of senior managers decrease after they have left the bankrupt firm. The average age of the departing manager is only 52, so accumulated reductions in earnings over their remaining worklife should be sizable.

Apart from sanctions by the managerial labor market, the management may suffer a loss of prestige, reputation, and nonpecuniary benefits, since control over the firm'' assets is shifted to creditors. These latter losses are hard to measure empirically, but Gilson [1989, 1990] is also offering some empirical and anecdotal evidence for reputational losses and concrete reductions in managerial wealth.

Against the background of these personal cost, theoretical analysis attributes properties to debt, which equity capital is said to be lacking. For example, some representatives of capital structure theory based on conflicts between shareholders and management postulate that debt can provide incentives to managers, who want to avoid the unpleasant effects of bankruptcy. Likewise, capital structure theories based on asymmetric information also rely on these

---

[10] Fama uses the fitting analogy of a sports coach. "The manager of a firm, like the coach of any team, may not suffer any immediate gain or loss in current wages from the current performance of his team, but the success of failure of the team impacts his future wages, and this gives the manager a stake in the success of the team." (Fama [1980, 292]).

personal cost as an important part of their argument. In those models, management increases firm leverage in order to signal favorable information about the firm's earning prospects in order to gain advantageous treatment by the capital markets. Debt financing can help to overcome asymmetric information, since it is more attractive to those firms whose earning prospects are truly good. This argument is based on the idea that a given leverage will expose the management of a good firm to a lower risk of financial distress than that of a bad firm.

1.3 Theories of Capital Structure

Now that we have taken a look on the two financial instruments, we are in a position to review the existing informational theories of capital structure. The selection of articles is of course biased in the sense that we have chosen contributions that serve as a starting point to our own work in Chapters 2 to 4. In order to see what role capital structure is playing, it is sometimes necessary to understand what role it is not playing. Because of that and for reasons of completeness we will also review some approaches which are not directly related to our own field of interest. For an exhaustive overview over informational theories of financing we refer to the articles by Harris and Raviv [1991, 1992]. The theories reviewed are – as in Harris and Raviv [1992] – allotted to four different categories, to which we have added a fifth one, which was still in its infancy when Harris and Raviv wrote their article. Each of the following Sections will start with some general comments concerning the underlying informational friction before the literature based on this friction is addressed.[11] Informational frictions are often analyzed by making the agreement between parties involved explicit in the form of a contract. Such a contract is not to be understood as a contract in the legal sense, but rather as the formalization of a convention made at the beginning of the relationship.

The literature review is now set up as follows: We will first turn to capital structure theories based on principal-agent (or agency) problems. Next come

[11] For a detailed exposition of Informational Economics consult Hillier [1997] or Salanié [1997].

financing theories of asymmetric information. In the third Section we will turn to models of corporate control, which are mainly drawing on signaling models. This will be followed by a fourth Section of financing theories based on the theory of industrial organization, which is relying on the whole spectrum of models in informational economics and game theory. A fifth and last Section addresses models of incomplete contracts, which are in fact a variety of the principal-agent framework with an additional complication.

1.3.1 Agency

Agency problems can arise whenever one person is acting on behalf of another person. Due to the division of labor in modern society, economic agents often hire other agents with superior knowledge or skills, since many tasks can be performed better by a specialist than by an economic agent who does not possess any special knowledge. This strategic relationship basically consists of one party (called the principal) which is delegating tasks to another party (called the agent), whose further action affects the utilities of both players.

It may be impossible specify the action of the agent in the initial contract, since this action is either *unobservable* (i.e. private information to the agent) or *unverifiable*. The first expression means that the principal can literally not see the action of the agent.[12] The second expression means that the principal cannot enforce such an agreement, since a third party cannot verify what the agent's action has been. this is for instance the case if the principal observes what the agent is doing, but cannot prove in court that the agent infringes the terms of the contract.

The delegation does not cause any problems in standard neoclassical models according to which agents are by assumption perfectly loyal. Once an employee has agreed to the terms of employment, he can be forced to take the action for which he was hired. Compared to reality however, this view is often too simplistic. Monitoring an agent to ensure that he indeed holds his promise can be very costly or even impossible. If the very reason for hiring an agent was his

[12] Throughout the book we will refer to the principal as "she" and to the agent as "he".

superior knowledge, observing his actions may not tell the principal whether these actions are appropriate. But then, instead of performing his task in the principal's best interest, the agent may rather be led by self-interest and not keep to the contract he should feel bound to.

Principal-agent theory, as represented by Holmström [1979] or Hart and Holmström [1983], provides a framework to analyze economic situations that are contaminated with the friction just described. The agent performs an unobservable (or unverifiable) task for a principal which results in an verifiable output. There is symmetric information about all characteristics of the model before parties enter into the contractual relationship, but the agent holds private information after he has taken his action. This does not cause any problems as long as there is a deterministic relationship between his action and the verifiable output, since it is then possible to derive his input from this variable. The informational friction becomes important if the agent's final performance is stochastically co-determined by some random variable. This makes it impossible to draw an exact conclusion about the agent's input from merely observing the final performance. If the principal wants to elicit a certain behavior from her agent, she must provide him with incentives, that induce him to show that behavior voluntarily. This is in general achieved by burdening the agent with consequences of his action, i.e. he participates in success and failure.[13] A branch of the literature on capital structure has argued that principal-agent problems play a prominent role for the firm's choice of financing.

In many corporations, ownership of assets and control over these assets are not concentrated in one hand, but they are rather divided between several institutions and securityholders. It has long been recognized that this "separation of ownership and control" (Fama and Jensen [1983a]) may involve incentive problems, which originate from the fact that the party who is in charge of the firm's operating decisions does not bear the entire wealth effect of these

[13] For further details on principal-agent theory see Hart and Holmström [1987], Kreps [1990], Fudenberg and Tirole [1992] or Salanié [1997].

decisions.[14] The problem is essentially a problem stemming from economic agents' specialization in certain activities. While investors provide the firm's funding, a manager with superior human capital is employed to take the firm's operating decisions. The management's unique skills may be one reason to delegate control. Another reason might be that ownership among investors is too dispersed to let them all take part in the decision process.

Given that the manager is only an employee of the firm, "his incentive to devote significant effort to creative activities such as searching out new profitable ventures" (Jensen and Meckling [1976, 313]) is not as intense as in the situation in which he internalizes all returns from investment. A manager might therefore "avoid such ventures simply because it requires too much trouble or effort on his part to manage or to learn about new technologies" (Jensen and Meckling [1976, 313]). The agency conflict is not necessarily limited to the management's willingness to work hard. it could just as well consist of the manager's diversion of funds to projects, which have nothing to do with productive investment, but with an idiosyncratic preference of the management's. Moreover, the conflict is not restricted to the relationship between management and shareholders. Agency problems can literally arise between all parties involved into the firm's business.

We will now review some contributions to the theory of capital structure which start from agency conflicts as a determining force. Harris and Raviv [1992] provide a detailed survey on these theories and we refer the interested reader to this reference for an exhaustive presentation of the literature.

Jensen and Meckling [1976]

Jensen and Meckling [1976] are the first authors who explicitly adopt an agency perspective on capital structure. Instead of using the term capital structure, they refer to ownership structure. While capital structure is denoting the relative quantities of debt and equity, ownership structure points to another dimension

---

[14] Adam Smith is one of the first authors to recognize the problem (see the motivating citation in Jensen and Meckling [1976, 305]). Later references are Berle and Means [1932] and more recently Jensen and Meckling [1976], Fama [1980] plus Fama and Jensen [1983b].

of the financing decision, namely the importance of different claim structures on the return streams of the firm. The main focus of their paper is to spot the different agency conflicts, as they arise in a relationship between an owner-entrepreneur and a financier.

If the manager is the sole owner of the firm, he will bear the full cost of any slackness or the consumption of perquisites. In this situation the owner will trade off the personal cost of slackness against his personal benefits. This trade-off is disturbed as soon as he partially gives up ownership to stockholders. With partial outside equity financing, a principal-agent conflict arises between management and equityholders.

When the manager is not full residual claimant of the firm's return stream, consuming private benefits at the expense of monetary benefits will be more attractive, because he enjoys all benefits of such a policy, without bearing the full cost.

A second type of agency conflict may arise between equityholders and creditors because of the special design of both securities. Equityholders determine the investment strategy and are residual claimants of the receipts in excess of debt repayments. Given some debt financing, equityholders (or managers as their representatives) might find it attractive to invest money into a very risky project that generates a huge payoff with a small probability, while it results in financial distress with a relatively large probability. If the project succeeds, equityholders capture most of the gains while in case of a failure creditors are bearing most of the cost.[15]

The cost associated with these agency conflicts will finally be borne by the manager-entrepreneur, who is issuing the financial securities. Outside equityholders – when valuing the stock – will take management's hazardous behavior into account, while creditors will anticipate any risky behavior and ask for a compensation. The authors make some remarks on issues of diversification, which could favor outside financing in excess of the minimum

[15] Baums [1994, 414] has put this into the pointed phrase "Heads I win, tails you loose".

amount necessary, but otherwise the firm should rely as little on outside financing as possible in order to minimize agency cost (see Jensen and Meckling [1976, 345]).[16]

The only means to minimize the agency cost of financing in Jensen and Meckling [1976] is the financing mix. What they completely ignore are other devices such as auditing, monitoring or incentive compensation. This seems to be the weak point of their analysis. The mix of debt and equity gains importance only, because other devices, which could limit these cost (maybe even more effectively), are ruled out. However the seminal contribution of Jensen and Meckling is the application of agency theory to the theory of financial structure. While Modigliani and Miller [1958] assume that the firm's return stream is independent of its financial structure, Jensen and Meckling provide an argument which just on the contrary emphasizes the role of financing for the value of the firm.

Grossman and Hart [1982]

The model by Grossman and Hart [1982] is fundamentally different regarding the role capital structure is playing. While in the model of Jensen and Meckling, capital structure is chosen to minimize the agency cost of financing, debt serves as an incentive device here. As we have seen above, bankruptcy can cause management specific cost, like reputational cost, cost related to job search or foregone future income. The general idea of this paper is that debt financing can rouse management's interest in high profits. In order to keep expected bankruptcy cost low, management will seek to take actions which minimize the risk of bankruptcy induced by debt financing. Both parties (shareholders and management) are then interested in high profits, though for different reasons. Even though the authors recognize that other mechanisms have the potential to alleviate the conflict in interest between management and shareholders, they

[16] Many graphical arguments in the original article remain vague, since Jensen and Meckling do not spell out an explicit utility function for the manager. The book by Barnea, Haugen and Senbet [1985] exclusively deals with agency problems related to the financing of the firm and clarifies many of those issues.

disregard (as Jensen and Meckling) the most obvious of those devices, namely an incentive compensation schedule.

The model puts forward an owner-manager of a firm, who must raise all funds necessary to pay for the initial investment either by borrowing or issuing shares. The management derives utility from funds diverted to the consumption of perks. That is, rather than investing the raised funds into production, management may consume perks, which are not of any value to investors. Management can only enjoy these perks as long as the firm is not in financial distress. given that a certain sum of money has been supplied by the capital market, and given that a certain fraction of this sum is raised by debt, there is a trade-off for the manager. Putting the money into productive investment will lower the sum which is left over for the consumption of perks, but this will also decrease the probability of financial distress. On the other hand, he may waste the money (from the viewpoint of investors) by spending it on perks. That way, he increases the amount of consumed perks, but the probability of keeping them goes down.

Financial markets cannot observe the management's investment (or equally the funds diverted), but they can make inferences from the capital structure chosen by the management. As a result, the value of the firm will not be independent of the debt equity ratio. Capital structure is playing the role of a precommitment or bonding device in this model. If management went on to finance investment completely by equity, financial markets would anticipate the management's strong incentives to divert funds rather than to invest them. If the manager took on just a little bit of debt, he would alter his incentives in the trade-off described. His maximization problem is to choose debt financing so as to maximize his expected utility from the consumption of perks. In equilibrium, the total amount of money raised, capital structure and investment (and thus the consumption of perks) are determined.

Grossman and Hart [1982] are the first authors to providc a closed theory of capital structure as an incentive device. In Jensen and Meckling [1976] the financial structure gains importance for the value of the firm through the minimization of agency cost related to the financing of the firm. Here, the debt-equity choice matters, since it is setting the incentives for the management to engage in an activity, which is not valued by investors. Both articles have in common that financing becomes relevant to the firm's valuation, because other devices which could help to alleviate the underlying incentive frictions are not taken into consideration.

Hart and Moore [1995]

The model of Hart and Moore [1995] borrows much from Jensen's free cash flow theory, first put forward in Jensen [1986]. Free cash flow describes funds left over after all available positive net-present-value projects have been carried out. Jensen identifies a conflict in interest between shareholders and management due to the fact that management prefers to engage in empire building rather than to pay out dividends to shareholders. The general idea is that management enjoys private benefits from managing the firm, which increase with the resources under control. For example, management might be inclined to promote the growth of the firm, rather than to pay out dividends, since its reputation is increasing corresponding to the size of the firm. According to Jensen [1986], debt can alleviate this problem by forcing the management to disgorge cash. If internal funds are withdrawn from management, new investment has to be financed by outside capital. As a consequence, management has to submit itself to the judgement of capital markets, which will deny funds if the project is not worthwhile undertaking.[17]

Hart and Moore [1995] present a theory of long-term debt financing based on Jensen's free cash flow argument. Their model has three stages. There are old assets in place at date one, which yield a return at date two and three. At date two a new investment project becomes available, which is requiring some investment expenditure and which promises a returns as of date three. The returns of old assets at that point are insufficient to fund this new investment, but management can borrow against future returns of new investment and

[17] See Blair and Schary [1993] or Mann and Sichermann [1991] on some empirical evidence concerning the free cash flow hypothesis.

returns of old assets. There is ex-ante uncertainty about the cost to set-up the new investment at date two, and there is ex-ante uncertainty about returns on old and new investment. This uncertainty is only resolved when the new investment opportunity becomes available. At that time, it becomes clear whether or not it is worthwhile to pursue the new project. Management will invest into the project if it is able to raise the necessary funds, and there is no mechanism whatsoever to stop such an investment. Specifically there is no incentive compensation available to realign interests. Contracts cannot be made contingent on the information whether the project is profitable or not. Therefore the only mechanism to prevent management to pursue a negative net-preset-value project is to make sure that management cannot raise a sufficient amount of money to set up the new project.
If the firm does not have any debt obligations, management will find it easy to raise funding for investment by borrowing against returns of assets in place. In consequence there is a risk of overinvestment. This risk can be limited by issuing claims senior to any newly issued ones. if future returns are already burdened with long term debt, it will be difficult to issue new claims, since existing long-term debt is higher in seniority. Debt financing thus brings about the risk of underinvestment. While Jensen [1986] stresses the benefits of debt in forcing the management to disgorge funds, Hart and Moore [1995] emphasize the possible cost, which can accrue if future returns are overmortgaged.[18]

Again, debt financing gains relevance only by abstracting from other mechanisms that could realign interests of management and shareholders. Management derives so much utility from even the most value decreasing investment, that it will rather waste money on silly projects instead of paying out dividends. The reason for taking on debt here is fundamentally different from the incentive reasons in Grossman and Hart [1982]. Debt is a brute force device for restricting management's squandermania.

---

[18] The brief presentation of the model has omitted a liquidation decision and a second type of debt (short-term debt) which both play a minor role in the model.

1.3.2 Asymmetric Information

Traditional neoclassical theory has little to say about situations in which some market participants hold better information than others. However, the assumption that all agents can observe equally well the characteristics of all commodities and other agents, often fails to give a good picture of the real word. Reality is rather crammed with situations in which agents interact on the basis of asymmetric information. For example, a seller of a good may be better informed about the quality of the good to be sold than a potential buyer, or an individual may have better information about his health than a life-insurance company. The dissatisfaction with this unrealistic assumption contributed a good deal to the development of informational economics, which allows to address this kind of friction.

Akerlof [1970] – one of most cited works from the early days of informational economics – deals with the problem of asymmetric information in a market for used cars. While sellers are perfectly aware of the state their car is in, potential buyers do not have this information. Not being informed about the quality of an individual car, they have only an idea about the average quality in the market. This informational asymmetry does not cause any problems as long as a buyer and seller can write costlessly enforceable contracts specifying the price for a car of certain quality.

If the buyer is unable to find out about this characteristic, the price of the car cannot depend on quality. As a severe consequence of the impossibility to specify a traded car's quality, markets can break down. This may happen since a price change can have side effects, which are absent in the traditional neoclassical theory. There, the price mechanism will (under certain conditions) bring about an allocation, which is pareto-optimal by the first theorem of welfare economics. This mechanism may fail here, if sellers with good quality (and accordingly high reservation prices) successively leave the market as prices fall, thus altering the average quality of cars available. Buyers in turn will understand this relationship and reduce their demand in response to a price fall rather than to increase it.[19]

As a result, there may not exist a price at which trade takes place. Akerlof already points to a way out of this dilemma, but it is left to Spence [1973] to formalize this argument in an equilibrium framework. If sellers can engage in an activity that is more costly to a seller of a low quality car than to one of a higher quality, they can send signals to buyers, who can then draw conclusion about a car offered on the basis of the observed signal.[20] This activity must not make any productive contribution. Rather, this activity often results in being a mere waste of resources ("burning money").

It has been argued that asymmetric information among parties is an important determinant of the firm's capital structure decision. The theoretical variants of the friction have been transferred to the corporate financing literature in the form of many models from which we have chosen two consider as representative. Especially the signalling theory has been applied extensively to the financing context. Ross [1977] and Leland and Pyle [1977] are considered as the first references for this approach. We will give a brief sketch of the work by Ross [1977], which is essentially a transfer of Spence's [1973] job market signalling theory into the corporate finance world. Furthermore, we will present the model by Myers and Majluf [1984]. It is less relevant for our own work, but we mention it here because of its fundamentally different outlook on capital structure.

[19] For a formal presentation of the argument see Eichberger [1993, pp. 169] and Tirole [1988, pp. 108].

[20] Such an activity could be the promise to pay for any repair of the car in a given time. This promise would be more costly to a seller of a low quality car, if such a car is more likely to break down during the guarantee period. Spence [1973] does not use Akerlof's example of a market for used cars, but he makes his point in a labor market setting. There, an agent can choose his education to send a signal about his ability, which is unobserved by potential employers.

Ross [1977]
A manager with inside information on his firm's cash flow distribution can take on debt to signal his superior knowledge to the capital markets. The management of a good firm (in the sense that the distribution over this firm's cash flow dominates that of a bad form in the sense of first-order stochastic dominance) has an interest to communicate its private knowledge to capital markets, since it is rewarded for a higher valuation of the firm via compensation. This compensation does not play any role in the model apart from inducing a managerial interest in a high valuation of the firm. Ross [1977, 28] postulates that a management suffers bankruptcy cost of L if it fails to service outstanding debt. On this basis, debt financing is able to serve as a signalling device, since engaging in debt financing is less costly for a manager of a good firm than for that of a bad firm. There is no production decision for management to be made, but the only decision is the choice of capital structure, which does not have any real effects here.

The case is different in another branch of the asymmetric information literature as it is applied to the theory of capital structure. Inefficiencies of the Akerlof type can be overcome by choosing an appropriate financing mix and thus, capital structure can have real effects. The work of Myers and Majluf is a model of this type.

Myers and Majluf [1984]
In this model, a firm with assets in place is considering to issue new shares to finance some further investment. Firm insiders are better informed than potential investors about the total returns of old and new assets, and prospective new investors will therefore ask for a reduction in the share price to account for the possibility that earning perspectives are in fact bad. Just as socially desirable trade might fail in Akerlof's model, it can be the case that insiders forgo a positive net present value investment project here. Outsiders participate in total returns by acquiring claims in the firm, or, expressed differently, insiders give up claims to the total cash flow, when issuing new shares.

Outside investors acquire two different claims when investing into the firm. On the one hand they acquire a partial claim in the existing assets, and, on the other hand, they acquire claims in the new investment. If the return share captured in old investment is relatively high, insiders might be well advised to let the new investment opportunity pass, if they have to pay for its implementation by giving up too much claims. Financing new investment through internal funds will, of course, circumvent the problem altogether, but if internal funds are insufficient, the firm has to turn to outside financing. Issuing debt avoids the disadvantage of letting outsiders participate in existing assets returns. Thus, it might become possible to install some investment project, which would be ignored if shareholders could finance new investment by issuing new shares only.

The model provides an argument to explain why firms tend to prefer retained earnings over debt and debt financing over issuing equity when financing their investment. Myers [1984] has coined the term "pecking order" for this pattern.

1.3.3 Corporate Control

Theories in this approach are built on the voting rights attached to securities. Voting rights are an important determinant of who controls the firm in non-bankrupt states. This is why the capital structure decision can be of high interest to management, current shareholders, or outsiders, who want to buy the firm. In a takeover, ownership of the firm is transferred to some outsider, who often changes management and firm policies. One can distinguish several types of takeovers, depending on whether it is resisted by the incumbent management (hostile takeover) or not (merger), whether the takeover is mainly financed by debt (leveraged buy-out), or by whom the takeover is led (e.g. management buy-out). The success or failure of such transactions is heavily influenced by the capital structure of the targeted firm. Models taking this approach center around the question of how the distribution of gains in such a transaction can be influenced (Israel [1991]), or how the probability of a takeover is influenced by different choices of capital structure (Harris and Raviv [1988]).

One of the prominent roles attributed to takeovers is to remedy inefficient behavior of target firms. If a management does not put the assets at their most productive use, other management teams will recognize this inefficiency and try to acquire the firm, since there is a gain to be made. The existence of this device thus has the potential to alleviate agency conflicts as described above. For the reason just mentioned, Jensen [1986] sees takeovers as a socially desirable mechanism to assign control to the management team with the highest ability. Since we do not take this approach in our own contributions, we do not present a specific model in detail here. We do however come back to takeovers, when we put the firm's financial decision into the broader framework of corporate governance mechanisms in Section 4 of this Chapter.

1.3.4 Industrial Organization

The theory of industrial organization studies firm behavior and the functioning of markets in the context of various industries. In addition to the classical pricing and quantity decision, it is dealing with advertizing, research and development, product differentiation and many other strategic aspects of the firm's activity.[21] As an empirical observation, firms in the same industry tend to have similar financing patterns (e.g. see Blair and Schary [1993] or Spence [1985]). This observation led financial economists to believe that factors beyond the underlying information structure have an impact on this decision as well. These determinants could have something to do with the product itself, the special production process of the industry, the generic relationship between providers of inputs to the production process, or finally with matters of competition.

Financing theories drawing on the theory of industrial organization do not rely on one single informational friction, but they are using virtually any model from game theory or informational economics to explain observed financing patterns in various industries. For that reason, opponents sometimes blame the approach to produce ad hoc theories, but in every case it has the major advantage over

[21] For a thorough treatment of the theory with an exposition of the topics just mentioned we refer to Tirole [1988] or more recently Shy [1995].

many other theories, in that it can be tested empirically quite well on grounds of the predictions generated. This is often difficult to do for more abstract theories, like the agency or the asymmetric information approach presented above.

Research in this field started with an article by Brander and Lewis [1986], which analyzes the linkage of financial and product markets in a simple Cournot duopoly setting. We are aware that our choice of contributions to this line of research leaves out many interesting recent financing theories based on the theory of industrial organization, but the fact that models are scattered over too many different types of theoretical approaches prevents us from giving even a modest overview here.[22]

Brander and Lewis [1986]

Before the work of Brander and Lewis [1986] the financing literature had already established theories of how the capital structure could impact the firm's cash flow by influencing an underlying informational friction. But until then, there had apparently been a dichotomy between financial and real decisions in the sense that financial decisions were held not to have any consequences for the strategic interaction with other firms. The model by Brander and Lewis is the first one to give a theoretical underpinning for the linkage of financial and product markets in the sense that the firm's financing decision has an impact on its own production decision and the production decision of competitors. The basic idea of the model is that a firm can commit itself to a more aggressive output strategy by relying on debt financing. As we will see shortly, the model mirrors the agency conflict between debtholders and equityholders identified by Jensen and Meckling [1976].

---

[22] Among them are the approach represented by Bronars and Deere [1991] and Perotti and Spier [1991], who view capital structure as a device to improve on shareholders' bargaining position in negotiations with workers or unions. Another approach, taken for example by Erlei and Schmidt-Mohr [1995] or by Harris [1994], in which the asset specifity is identified as a determinant for the firm's financing choice, is dating back to Williamson [1988]. For some further reference on the theory of capital structure as it relates to the theory of industrial organization, the reader is referred to the overview article by Maksimovic [1995].

Brander and Lewis use a Cournot duopoly framework, in which two firms compete in a market for a homogeneous product. The model has two stages. in a first stage, firms simultaneously make their financing decision, while, in the second stage, they simultaneously decide on the quantity to produce. Each firm's profit is determined by the two quantities chosen and, apart from that, by a firm specific random variable, which is capturing the uncertainty of the firm's business. Financial decisions are assumed to be taken before quantity decisions, which are in turn made before the uncertainty is resolved. Marginal profitability increases with the realization of the random variable, i.e. a firm will want to produce more output for higher realizations of the random variable. Since the output decision has to be made before the realization becomes known, the firm must base its decision on a probability distribution over the continuous support of the random variable.

Each firm must service its debt obligation out of the cash flow which is available at the end of its time, and it might well be the case that a firm goes bankrupt if the random variable takes on some realization below a critical value. The critical value below which equityholders do not receive any return increases in the debt level chosen, i.e. equityholders are residual claimants for fewer and fewer states as debt financing increases. Since marginal profitability goes up with the realization of the random variable, equityholders will prefer to choose a higher output than debtholders before uncertainty is resolved. This is the case since equityholders are protected by limited liability which causes that only non-bankrupt states (i.e. high realizations of the random variable) are relevant to them. It turns out that management – on behalf of equityholders – will maximize the return to equity by successively choosing higher output levels as debt increases. Increased debt levels leave successively higher states to be relevant for equityholders and given that such a realization is taken on, equityholders will prefer to produce a high output, since then marginal profit is high also. Thus, returns in non-bankrupt states are boosted at the expense of lowering those in bankrupt states even further.

There is a second (negative) effect related to the agency conflict between equityholders and debtholders which is arising here. If debtholders are rational, they will anticipate that debt financing is exploited as a strategic device to commit to some output strategy. But then, debt will be priced accordingly and extra debt financing will – from some point on – be value decreasing for the firm in spite of the positive strategic effect. The optimal capital structure is found here as the trade-off between these two conflicting effects. As a general result, the equilibrium on the output market will be influenced by both firms' choice to finance itself. If the two competitors use the commitment device of debt, the output equilibrium will be characterized by a higher aggregate output as compared to the situation in which this device is not available. As a result both firms will be worse off.[23]

Poitevin [1989]

Poitevin [1989] does not rely on a conflict in interest between debt- and equityholders, but his contribution is in the tradition of the signaling approach as represented by Ross [1977]. The model is a representative of the literature which postulates a link between product markets and financial markets on the basis of predatory practises. Those practises involve means such as temporarily setting low prices or dumping in order to drive competing firms out of the market or to discourage their entry in the first place. Tirole [1988, pp. 367] is giving an overview over the predation literature.

Poitevin's article formalizes the so-called "deep-pocket" or "long-purse" argument attributed to Telser, which is extensively presented in Tirole [1988, 377]. The argument goes that a firm which faces a tight constraint to raise capital is vulnerable against predatory practices of a second firm which does not face such a constraint. By charging low prices, the second firm can impose losses upon the financially constrained firm which might have to exit the market as a result, or which might decide not to enter the market initially.

In Poitevin [1989] there are two firms, one incumbent and one potential entrant. Before firms compete in a market for a homogeneous product, they must finance setup cost $K > 0$. Financiers are uncertain concerning the entrant's

[23] Brander and Lewis [1988] and Brander and Spencer [1989] are additional reference that further develop the idea of Brander and Lewis [1986].

marginal cost of production and, as a result, its securities cannot directly be priced on the basis of its true cost. The model is set up in two stages. Both firms have to finance their fixed production cost at an initial stage (financial stage) before they compete in a Cournot manner during a second stage (output stage). Both Cournot profits are (additively) affected by a random shock such that a firm can default on its debt taken on in the first stage. A non-bankrupt firm derives an exogenous benefit $B > 0$ from bankruptcy of its opponent. One can view this benefit as an increment in firm value due to the monopoly position of the firm in (unmodelled) future periods. This benefit creates a link between the firms' output decision and the financial decisions taken in the first stage. Since a firm receives a benefit if its competitor defaults on its debt level, it will take the competitor's financial policy into account when making its output decision.

A potential entrant will prefer equity financing since it does not want to elicit predatory practices from the competitor in the second stage. However, in order to communicate its type, a low-cost entrant may have to engage into some debt financing to achieve an appropriate pricing of its securities within financial markets. Taking on debt is more costly to high-cost entrants than to low-cost entrants and, therefore, this activity has the potential to sort among types. Debt financing will expose the entering firm to the risk of bankruptcy in the output stage, and the incumbent may well be successful in driving the entrant out of the market again. The model predicts an increase in the incumbent's quantity as a response to debt financing of the entrant. This is the major difference to the work of Brander and Lewis [1986]. in their model, it is the leveraged firm which increases its quantity, while in Poitevin's model, it is the unleveraged firm which is increasing its quantity in response to its opponents increase in debt.[24]

[24] Fulghieri and Nagarajan [1996] is very similar to the model of Poitevin [1989] in the sense that the incumbent will also have an incentive to engage in predatory practises for pre-emptive reasons.

Glazer [1994]
In contrast to Brander and Lewis [1986], the model of Glazer [1994] predicts that debt financing can lead to softer market competition. While the models of Fulghieri and Nagarajan [1996] and Poitevin [1989] rely on predatory practises as the connecting link between financial markets and product markets, Glazer's argument does not involve such practises. Glazer does not explicitly model the choice of capital structure, but his interesting result is that the strategic effect of debt financing might just be the opposite of the theoretical predictions just described.

His model is, roughly speaking, a two stage version of Brander's and Lewis' model. two firms interact twice on a market for a homogeneous product, and both have to repay a certain debt level out of accumulated profits at the end of the second period. The second period is identical to Brander and Lewis [1986] in the sense that output market behavior will be the more aggressive the higher the outstanding debt. When making an output decision in period 1, a firm will take into consideration that its competitor will act the more aggressively in period 2 the lower its profits in period 1 have been. In anticipation of this fact, firm 1 will avoid to inflict low earnings on its competitor initially. This will cause the competitor to have relatively high earnings in the first period, which again will induce moderate competition in the second stage.

1.3.5 Incomplete Contracts

In all of the models presented above financing gained its relevance by abstracting from other mechanisms such as monetary compensation. This insufficiency has been recognized and there is one approach – the incomplete contracts approach to financial structure – which (at least partially) addresses this issue. Before we present the model which laid the foundation for this branch of literature, we first need to make some general remarks on the theory of incomplete contracts.

The issue of control in the traditional theory of the firm, i.e. the question who is exercising power over the firm's assets, is not of any interest, because economic agents enter into a comprehensive contract before their economic interaction takes place. The initial contract deals with breach of contract, fraud or any opportunistic behavior on behalf of the agent. Principal-agent theory has allowed for an explicit modelling of conflicts of interest between management and a second party (e.g. owner, creditor, worker), yet still and perhaps surprisingly, who controls the firm is not really an issue. Even though contracts cannot specify a certain action, they can be made contingent on verifiable output and induce a certain behavior of the agent.

The principal is perfectly aware of her manager's behavior, since she has designed his incentive framework. Delegation of control is definitely associated with certain cost originating from the underlying incentive frictions, but after the principal has set the framework, her agent is only a marionette on the strings of the incentive scheme. In general, the allocation of control rights (or the rights to set the contracts governing the mutual behavior) may affect the parties payoff, but it has no consequences for efficiency.[25] The notion of control in the sense of Hart [1988a] and Aghion and Bolton [1989, 1992] is fundamentally different from discretionary decision rights in principal agent-models and goes beyond the scope of some hidden-action scenario. Now, the issue is not only to induce the agent to take some action desired by the principal, but rather to assign control (i.e. who is allowed to decide what) in the first place.

Contracts in the definition of Aghion and Bolton [1992] are incomplete as soon as they do not give precise provisions for every future event and thus allow for pareto-improving renegotiation.[26] Different to the standard hidden-action scenario in which parties cannot contract upon the agent's effort choice, incompleteness of contracts is about including specific states of nature in the contract. Since contracts cannot be written on each possible future event, some

[25] Many principal-agent models think about the contract design problem in the following way: maximize the principal's utility, while holding the agent's utility at a constant level. This of course, generates a Pareto-optimal allocation, but holding the principal's utility at a constant level and maximizing the agent's utility instead generates such an allocation as well.

[26] For recent surveys on incomplete contracts see Tirole [1995] and furthermore Salanié [1997, chapter 7]. Hart [1988b] is considered as one of the seminal articles, which started the discussion on incomplete contracts related to the theory of the firm.

important contingencies are left out of the initial contract. Yet, some decision must be made by somebody if such a state realizes.

This is where capital structure comes in. In a world of incomplete contracts, the debt-equity choice can matter because it specifies a governance structure, i.e. who is allowed to decide what to do in an unspecified event. In a fully equity financed firm, shareholders are in control in any contingency that can possibly arise. Equally, a bank can be called upon to decide, if there is debt financing involved. Mixes of those alternatives can induce different governance structures depending on the realization of stochastic cash flow. We shall now present the model by Aghion and Bolton [1992] which has started the literature taking an incomplete contract view on the theory of capital structure. They analyze what the device of capital structure can contribute to an efficient control allocation among parties involved into an investment project.

A penniless owner of a family business has to turn to a wealthy investor for the funding of a project, which yields two kinds of benefits. On the one hand, there are verifiable monetary benefits, which can be distributed among the parties according to a sharing rule. On the other hand, there is a non-verifiable, non-contractible and non-transferable private benefit, which is exclusively accruing to the manager-owner. Since he is wealth restricted, there is no way to take these benefits away from him. The height of both benefits depends on the realization of a state s, which is non-contractible. for each state of nature s, there is a socially optimal action in the sense that it maximizes the sum of both benefits. Assigning control to one party does not necessarily fix the implemented action at that one which is maximizing this parties utility. Instead, the other party may attempt to influence this choice in a renegotiation process, after s has realized. All the bargaining power is (initially and in any renegotiations) with the wealth restricted owner-entrepreneur, such that the investor can only hope for her reservation utility payoff.

If private benefits are comonotonic in total revenues, there is no conflict in interest, since the entrepreneur's most preferred action in this case is identical with the investor's most preferred action. The situation is acquiring interest if private benefits are not comonotonic with total revenues. Assigning the decision right to the investor will sometimes result in socially suboptimal action choices, because she cares about monetary benefits only, and the wealth restricted entrepreneur is unable to compensate her for any choice which increases private benefits at the expense of monetary returns. On the other hand, entrepreneur control might not reach first-best as well, if he demands a higher bribe to take a socially optimal action than it is worth to the investor.

The big difference to standard hidden-action models is that even second-best might not be reached, even though monetary compensation is available. Ordinary monetary incentives can fail to do the job here, if the monetary transfer to the entrepreneur necessary to induce the investor's most preferred action is so high that it is not worthwhile for the investor to agree to such a sharing rule, be it ex-ante or in a renegotiation process. Moreover, an investor might not be willing to finance a project with entrepreneur control, since she anticipates that she will be deprived of her returns. Thus, the only way to implement a project might be to assign control to the investor, who will in some situations choose socially suboptimal actions.

Apart from the unilateral control in which the decision right is assigned to either one of the two parties, there is a second type of control, the so-called contingent control. This type assigns control to one of the parties contingent on the realization of some contractible random variable, which is correlated with the non-contractible random variable s. if the variables are perfectly correlated, the contractual incompleteness disappears. Of course this case is trivial, since then a comprehensive contract can be written to implement the socially optimal action. But even an imperfect relationship can be exploited to overcome the contractual incompleteness. The essence of contingent control is that it is more flexible in the sense that it assigns control to whatever party is most likely to take the socially optimal action. It may thus pareto-dominate any unilateral control setting.

Unilateral control is a very natural type of control. Contingent control in contrast seems to be highly stylized at first. However, it turns out that debt financing can be interpreted as a kind of contingent control assignment. If control could be made contingent on the state of nature, it should be allocated to whatever party is taking the first best action. But since this is impossible, contracts are written on some verifiable signal. This signal is imperfectly correlated with an unverifiable one and thus, a first-best scenario may be approximated. In a sense, contingent control is a new view on the stylized fact that control is assigned to a firm's creditors when profits are low (possibly in the state of bankruptcy), and to the entrepreneurs or management when profits are high.

A strange feature of contingent control is that shifts in control are not triggered by the failure to make a debt repayment, but just by the realization of a verifiable random variable. The model is thus rather a theory to explain shifts in control than a theory of debt financing, as claimed by the authors. Even though the authors show that financial structure (with its special emphasis on control rights) can improve on efficiency, they fail to show why capital structure (with its special emphasis of debt versus equity financing) can perform better than monetary incentives in limiting managerial misbehavior.

The article by Berglöf [1994] has adopted this framework to model a venture capital relationship, in which capital structure is designed so as to alleviate distributional effects of a future sale of the firm. The main role of capital structure in this model is again to safeguard a financier's fund invested into the firm. Dewatripont and Tirole [1994] present a model in which the financial structure of the firm complements traditional incentive schemes in disciplining the management. As in the paper by Aghion and Bolton [1992], monetary compensation as such is not able to control the management.[27]

1.4 Corporate Governance Mechanisms

According to the definition of Shleifer and Vishny [1997, 737], corporate governance "deals with the ways in which suppliers of finance to corporations

---

[27] For a survey on financial contracting related to the theory of incomplete contracts see the book by Hart [1995].

assure themselves getting a return on their investment". This is an important issue, since many corporations have delegated the operational decisions to a professional management, or, to put it differently, "[shareholders] part with their money and have little to contribute afterwards" (Shleifer and Vishny [1997, 737]). In general, corporate governance mechanisms are legal and economic institutions, which safeguard fund providers' investment into the firm against the misbehavior of other parties involved into the firm's business. This includes any mechanism of control, bankruptcy laws, managerial compensation and the functioning of financial institutions through which funds are supplied to firms.

The reason why we dwell on this issue here is that capital structure is sometimes attributed a role in alleviating conflicts of interest between management and shareholders of the firm, as we have seen above (e.g. see the models by Grossman and Hart [1982] or the model by Hart and Moore [1995]). The relevance of this argument can only be assessed if one takes a look on the other mechanisms which are available. That way, one can gain an understanding of the interplay of capital structure with other corporate governance mechanisms. Since the corporate governance system of a country is in many respects mirrored in its financial system it is furthermore inevitable to give a brief exposition of the two generic financial systems.

Until now, we have only considered abstract informational frictions as the underlying determinant for a company's financial decision. This Subsection is supposed to direct attention to issues which are particularly related to the institutional environment the firm is operating in. If, apart from firm financing, there are other powerful governance mechanisms, one should expect that capital structure is only playing a subordinate role in securing shareholders' interests. On the other hand, there might be institutional characteristics that tend to promote the use of capital structure as a governance device. There are two main aims of this Subsection. Firstly, it seeks to obtain a broader perspective on capital structure by looking at other governance mechanisms. Secondly, it paves the way for our contribution in Chapter 3, which analyzes the firm's financial choice in the broader context of a financial system. Since space is limited, we are necessarily brief on many issues here. For further details on corporate governance, the interested reader is referred to the articles by Allen [1989], Myers [1989] or Shleifer and Vishny [1997] and the book by Blair [1995] or the one by Keasey, Thompson and Wright [1997].

We have chosen to arrange the different mechanisms into two groups. The first group – termed internal mechanisms – subsumes those mechanisms, which are directly controlled from within the firm. Examples are institutions like the board of directors, the corporate charter, the financing decision and incentive compensation schemes for the management. In contrast to that, the second group – termed external mechanisms – subsumes those mechanisms which are imposed on the firm from outside. It includes mechanisms as the market for corporate control, the product market and finally financial institutions and markets that monitor the firm from outside. As we will see, corporate governance mechanisms in both groups are intertwined, which often makes it difficult to analyze one mechanism without bringing into play another.

1.4.1 Internal Mechanisms

One obvious way to control management is to lay down rules in the corporate charter, to which this party must obey. It would harm the firm if managers were able to plunder the firm by selling its assets to a firm which they owned themselves. In general, the corporate charter can account for such outright fraud, but this device is too inflexible for more subtle cases of managerial misbehavior. For this reason, the corporate charter is only a very rudimentary way to protect shareholders' interests. A more flexible device would be to monitor management in some way. This is actually done by special institutions, which can be found in various types in different countries all over the world.

A management of a large public corporation in the US for example is complemented with the so-called board of directors which sets the general business policies and which is elected by shareholders, who thus indirectly participate in the firm'' decision process. Large German corporations are governed by a so-called two-tier board system consisting of the *Aufsichtsrat* and the *Vorstand*. The former of the two is composed of outside managers, which are (at least in theory) independent of actual firm managers on the *Vorstand* of the firm and who are intended to wield control over these managers.[28] These institutions are intended to grant shareholders a grip on firm management, but how successful they really are in limiting managerial misbehavior is questionable.

There is much debate on the benefits and drawbacks of such institutional systems especially with respect to recommendations to developing countries and the countries in Eastern Europe. Some argue that the German system is superior to the US system since it attempts to bring in firm outsiders to monitor managers, which is not done in the US system. Others argue that the German system is flawed by the fact that supervisory boards there are influenced by forces, such as labor unions, with goals different from those of investors. According to Emmons and Schmid [1998, 27], the composition of supervisory boards of the 100 largest German firms indeed sheds doubt on whether shareholders rights are protected through this institution. In 1993 there were 35% firm employees, 14% labor union executives, 27% retired or active executives of other firms and 9% bank representatives on it.

Another mechanism, which we have already mentioned several times, are incentive compensation schedules for those who influence the firm's economic fate most, top managers and chief executive officers (CEOs). This is a direct transfer of the insights gained through the application of principal-agent analysis to the theory of the firm. Top management compensation in many countries is consisting of a flat payment and an extra payment whose height depends on the success of the firm. This success dependent component can take on various forms. Phantom stock for example rewards the management for favorable stock movements with a bonus; stock-option plans assign call options to management and thus rouse managerial interest in stock price increases.

---

28 See Emmons and Schmid [1998] or Edwards and Fischer [1994] for an in depth presentation of the German system. Herzel [1987b] is a reference for details on the US and the UK system.

The success dependent percentage of management's pay makes up for a much bigger share in the Anglo-Saxon countries than, for example, in Japan or Germany, and, in general, incentive payment is not as widespread in central Europe as it is in the UK or the US.[29] This is puzzling since Brickley, Bhagat and Lease [1985] find a significant stock price increase for firms that announce to switch to a success dependent payment scheme.[30] While this evidence suggests that managerial remuneration is indeed playing a role for stockholders' valuation of the firm, Jensen and Murphy [1990] find evidence that is rather pointing to a weak relationship between CEO compensation and firm performance. Whatever the association between the two, incentive pay seems to play a more important role in the Anglo-Saxon countries as compared to Japan or central Europe. The underlying reason for these different weights on incentive pay may also be responsible for the different roles played by other mechanisms (such as financing) in countries' governance systems.[31]

According to our categorization the financing decision is an internal governance mechanism, since it can be controlled from within the firm. Taking on debt may play an incentive role as suggested by Grossman and Hart [1982], or it may force managers to disgorge funds, which would otherwise be used for negative net-preset-value projects (see Hart and Moore [1995]). Nevertheless, the financial choice of a company seems to bear most of its effects from outside. For example, product market competition is more of a threat to managers if they do have to fear to lose their jobs due to financial distress, and the market for corporate control might be in a position to discipline managers if the financing of the firm has been chosen diligently. A common argument in the corporate governance literature attributes a monitoring role to banks with respect to their client firms. If a bank is indeed performing such a task along with its business

[29] See Milgrom and Roberts [1992, pp. 410] for general comments on executive compensation in an international comparison and Kaplan [1994] for details on the case of Japan as compared to the US. Furthermore consult Herzel [1987a] and Greiler [1997] for information on executive compensation plans within German firms compared to the US.

[30] Similar evidence is found in Lewellen et al. [1992].

[31] For further theoretical and empirical details concerning executive compensation schedules consult Beck and Zorn [1982], Coughlan and Schmidt [1985] or Garvey, McCorry and Swan [1996].

to grant credit, investors' financing decision might e influenced by such considerations as well. We now turn to the raised issues in more detail.

1.4.2 External Mechanisms

Product Markets

Fama [1980] believes that "the firm is disciplined by competition from other firms, which forces the evolution of devices for efficiently monitoring the performance of the entire team and of its individual members" (Fama [1980, 289]). Incentive pay is playing a minor role in his view. If the firm'' assets are not put to their most productive use competition will drive the firm out of business or the market for corporate control will install a more skilled management team. Agency conflicts within the firm are therefore alleviated by competitive forces outside the firm.

Schmidt [1997] formalizes the idea that product market competition can have an impact on managerial incentives to the benefit of shareholders. His argument is based on managerial bankruptcy cost mentioned above. Product market competition is an important determinant of managerial incentives in his model, since, as Fama puts it, "the previous associations of a manager with success or failure are information about his talents" (Fama [1980, 292]). From that perspective, bankruptcy has the potential to affect the manager's discounted stream of earnings as was already described above. Schmidt derives conditions under which increased competition on product markets induces management to work harder. As such, product market competition can be seen as an external governance mechanism, which mitigates agency conflicts between management and shareholders of the firm.

Financial Systems

Apart from securities' return patterns, voting rights and bankruptcy considerations, the financial environment of the firm should be of high relevance to the financing decision. The firm issues its securities into an environment which perceives this decision differently depending on its structure and its institutions. In general, one can distinguish two different types of corporate financial systems. There is a bank-based system in which banks keep close relationships with firms while in the so-called market-based system this close relationship does not exist. Both systems have in common that firms' main source of financing are retained earnings, while financing via bank debt play a more important role in the former system.[32]

Japan and Germany are typically chosen as the representative countries for the former system, while the UK and the US are typically chosen as generic representatives for the market-based system. Apart from differences in the intensity of bank-firm relationships, a further distinguishing feature appears to be the development of financial markets. While the former system exhibits a relatively underdeveloped stock market, the latter on is characterized by sophisticated markets for all kinds of financial securities. The stress of this Subsection will be less on different financing patterns in the two systems than on different system-specific institutional arrangements which may influence a company's financial choice. In doing so, we will rather adopt a descriptive perspective but as we go along, we will also comment on what theory has to say about different institutions in the two systems.

An analysis of the financing decision in this broader framework has to look for characteristics of the specific environments, which have the potential to influence the firm's choice in one way or the other. In this sense the focus is more on financial institutions than on financial instruments. One question which is at the heart of this approach is whether banks can do something that anonymous markets for equity or bonds are not able to achieve.

The Bank-Based System Fama [1985] takes the view that a bank is in a better position than anonymous markets to provide funds to a firm, since it has a comparative advantage in gathering information about the corporate borrower. With a long standing relationship, the bank is aware of the deposit history and is well equipped in judging the firm's earning prospects. Fama does not provide any empirical evidence for his claim, but there is no doubt that bank-firm

[32] See Mayer [1988] for data concerning the financing patterns in different systems.

relations exist, and the role of banks in the bank-based system goes beyond that of a passive investor. Parallel to Fama, Cable [1985] argues that such close bank-firm relationships can help to overcome problems of credit rationing as described by Stiglitz and Weiss [1981] and may have the potential to systematically benefit countries' economic performance.[33]

A channel through which banks in the bank-oriented system could gain superior knowledge is their representation on client firms' supervisory boards. With respect to this representation, banks are commonly attributed a role in reducing conflicts of interest between management and other shareholders, who have typically less information on managerial effort and investment strategies. Adherents of this view usually adopt three interwoven arguments. These arguments are often made in a non-technical way, such that the exact chain of argumentation is remaining rather vague.

The first argument concerns the bank's role as a monitor of the firm in the widest sense. A classical example for this view is the paper by Aoki [1994], who attributes such a role to banks in the Japanese economy for several stages of the investment activity. According to him, monitoring of management may become necessary due to an informational asymmetry concerning the project's success probability, or due to hazardous behavior in the use of funds (see Aoki [1994, 111]). His theoretical underpinning for the ex-ante monitoring of a firm's project is similar to the work by Broecker [1990], who presents a model in which banks conduct a test of creditworthiness prior to a loan in order to keep the probability of failure to repay low.

A second, related argument, is that an intense relationship of a bank to the firm's business can help to overcome a free-rider problem in keeping an eye on firm management. This especially true if share ownership is too dispersed to make it worthwhile for any single shareholder to incur major monitoring cost. The bank is playing such a role in the model by Diamond [1984]. There, the financial intermediary does not have superior skills as compared to savers in the

[33] Edwards and Fischer [1994, 11] analyze UK and German GDP growth rates without verifying the content of this hypothesis for the case of both countries.

economy, but it is rather the case that monitoring is involving scale economies, implying that monitoring by one financial institution is more efficient than an independent monitoring of savers themselves.

As a third argument a bank may mitigate a prevailing conflict in interest between firm management and providers of funds through its representation on supervisory board, the control of voting rights and further devices, which allow the bank to interfere into managerial decision making. This reasoning is brought forward by Baums [1994, 413] and Cable [1985, 121] for the case of Germany and by Sheard [1989] for the case of Japan. Even though these contributions mention several ways in which the bank can influence the firm's policy, it remains unclear how the bank's close involvement should lead to fewer agency problems, and what the fundamental incentives to perform such a task are. In contrast to the second argument, it seems to be implicitly assumed that the bank has a comparative advantage in performing this task, be it through its specially trained staff on a firm's board or through its long standing relationship with the firm as a house bank with special insights into the firm's industry.

For the case of Germany, the close link between banks and firms manifests itself in a considerable supervisory board representation of banks. An argument which is quite frequently put forward by adherents of the bank-based financial system is the following one. Bank financing is said to avoid the anonymous market-based funding of investment, since "personal links may indeed help to mitigate conflicts between the firm and its managers or owners on one side and its creditor on the other side, and the advantages might exceed the cost of board representation" (Baums [1994, 417]). Since the supervisory board has an indirect influence on firm policy by appointing and is dismissing management, banks may theoretically guide firm policy through their representation on this institution.[34] In some cases, the supervisory board's consent with the firm's

[34] According to Edwards and Fischer [1994, 196], bank representation in 1978 accounted for 9.8% for all supervisory board members of the 100 largest German AGs, where some outstanding positions as the one of supervisory chairman or deputy chairman were held by bank employees.

product or market strategy is required, which may be a further possibility to limit managerial misbehavior.

The Japanese economy knows a specific form of close bank-firm linkages, the so-called *keiretsu*, a conglomerate of firms. At the center of this group is a so-called main bank which is providing financial services to group members and it is often a major shareholder of the firms. This close link is said to provide incentives for banks to engage in monitoring of the associated firms and it is especially seen to help to overcome problems of moral hazard and asymmetric information. *Keiretsu* is also seen to considerably lessen the mentioned free-rider problem, since the bank has strong incentives to monitor the creditors through its close involvement.

The Market-Based System These close ties to banks are not present in the market-based system of the UK or the US, and, maybe as a consequence, bank finance is not as pronounced in these countries as it is in Japan and several other countries in central Europe.[35] For the case of the US, it is tempting to explain the fact that close bank-firm relationships have not developed by the special legal framework which prevails there. US commercial banks are prohibited by law (through the Glass-Stegal Act) to engage in investment banking activities as it is common practise in Japan or Germany.

As a prominent empirical difference between the systems, firm ownership is dispersed amongst a large number of individuals in the UK and the US, while in Japan and Central Europe, ownership tends to be more concentrated; families or other corporate investors own significant fractions of a firm's stock.[36] One could think that an existing free-rider problem of controlling and monitoring should therefore be more severe in the UK and the US, since banks do not engage in any supervising activity. However, that would be wrong as there is

[35] See Mayer [1990] for an international perspective on the use of different sources of financing.

[36] Pagano and Röell [1998] note that in Italy about 75% of manufacturing firms are controlled by a single shareholder, while Zwiebel [1995, 161] notes that in 1981 the Fortune 500 corporations had on average only 1.4% of stockholders with blockholdings exceeding 5%. For data on Germany see the paper by Adams [1998] and the book by Edwards and Fischer [1994].

one governance mechanism which is particularly high developed in the market-based system.

Since common stock has voting rights attached, relying on this financial instrument exposes the firm to the risk that shares are acquired in such an amount that the current management is replaced by a new management. A takeover is such a transaction which is very often resisted by the incumbent management. This mechanism is said to benefit shareholders, since poorly performing managements can be removed from office and exchanged for a more skilled management, which is running the firm more diligently. In the UK and the US there are existing well developed markets for corporate control, which "subject quoted firms to a continuous auction process: whoever attaches the highest value to control has the right to bid for ownership" (Mayer [1987, 468]).

As banks are said to control the management in the bank-dominated system, takeovers threats are seen as a mechanism which is performing the task of control in Anglo-Saxon countries. A common argument blames the Anglo-Saxon system to be whortsighted in comparison to the bank-dominated system. opponents to this system argue that well chosen long-run strategies are sacrificed to the impatience of stockholders, who pressure the management into generating short-term profits. This is said not to be the case in the bank-based system. Takeovers combined with a resisted change in management are sparse in countries of continental Europe or Japan. In Germany, for example, hostile takeovers are virtually not existing.[37]

The financial system in the US knows a further mechanism, the existence of which is said to benefit shareholders by exercising control over the management. This mechanism is the so-called security class action, in which a group of small investors (the class) can sue the corporate officers and directors for a violation of their interests. This is a quite powerful threat to managers, since entrepreneurial lawyers have a high incentive to look for evidence on such

[37] Mayer [1987, 468] notes there have been only four cases of hostile (i.e. resisted) takeovers in Germany after World War II. See Jarrell, Brickley and Netter [1988] on empirical evidence concerning the market for corporate control in the US since the 1980s.

violations as they usually receive one-third of the damages. Strahan [1998] presents empirical evidence on this device.[38] Information on which a security class action can be based is easily accessible in the US. To be listed on a stock exchange, a firm must usually submit to certain accounting standards and show detailed balance sheet statements, which are intended to create transparency for potential investors. This will of course support the filing of such class actions.
As we have seen in the short discussion of both financial systems, the firm's financial choice may entail different governance implications, which might be a determining factor for investment finance. We have been rather short about many issues here, but we cannot elaborate this topic any further since it is not the main concern of analysis in this book. The interested reader is referred to Hellwig [1991] and Mayer [1988, 1990] for further remarks on the interaction of financial systems and the firm's decision to finance itself.

1.5 Scope of the Book

The book is subdivided into three core Chapters (Chapters 2 to 4) that present our own contributions, where each Chapter has a separate Appendix with proofs and technical details.

Chapter 2 explains the use of financial structure as an incentive device within a principal-agent model, where an investor has to delegate control over the firm's assets to a self-interested management. The investor cannot punish her manager arbitrarily hard by means of the monetary compensation schedule, since he is facing a limited liability constraint. If the manager wants to avoid financial distress since it is harmful to his human capital, financial structure may complement standard wage compensation schedules in providing incentives to management.

In excess of the classical role of financial intermediaries, banks are often attributed a role in mitigating an existing moral hazard problem between a self-interested management and equityholders. Chapter 3 embeds this argument into

[38] Shleifer and Vishny [1997, pp. 750] provide further comments on this mechanism and further legal protection of securityholders' interest in the US.

a formal framework. By taking on debt, the investor can induce the bank to exhibit an action which alleviates the prevailing friction originating from the unobservability of the management's effort. Bank activity is understood as bank representation on supervisory board and in general its supervision of firm management's decision in the course of firm business. The model shows that the bank's corporate governance activity can partially substitute for monetary incentives.

Chapter 4 adopts a signaling perspective on the choice of capital structure. We model the interaction of N firms in a Cournot manner and show that a firm can use its capital structure to signal its privately known marginal cost parameter to competitors. The choice of financing is affecting competitors' product market behavior via their beliefs. Thus, different sources of financing are not simply alternative ways to allocate claims to the firm's cash flow, but the financial choice might have real effects in the form of an altered product market behavior of opponent firms. Finally, Chapter 5 briefly summarizes our results.

Chapter 2

Capital Structure as an Incentive Device for a Wealth Constrained Management

2.1 Introduction

Separation of ownership and control in the course of a firm's business can lead to conflicts of interest between the firm owners and those who exercise control over the firm's asset on behalf of owners.[39] The modern corporation is likely to suffer from this problem, since its management usually holds an insignificant stake in the firm itself. Such a management will therefore only partially internalize the wealth effects of its decision and be inclined to take actions which owners dislike. Conflicts of interest are manifold and may arise in the form of a managerial aversion to work hard, as described in Jensen and Meckling [1976, 313], and modelled in Schmidt [1997], or it may take on the form of management's urge to waste firm resources as in Grossman and Hart [1982]. In order to regain goal congruence, firm owners can fall back on a large variety of mechanisms, e.g. monitoring devices, tournaments among subordinates, monetary remuneration, partial ownership in the business, fines for bad performance etc.[40]

The financial contracting literature has added the firm's financing to that list and argues that agency conflicts between management and firm owners can be resolved by diligently choosing the financing of the firm. This view has spawned a large body of literature contributing to the theory of capital structure,

---

[39] See chapter 1 for a detailed exposition on these issues.

[40] See the overview article by Gibbons [1997] on how these different devices function and furthermore FitzRoy and Kraft [1995] or MacLeod [1995] for related empirical work.

which is reviewed extensively in Harris and Raviv [1992]. Representatives for this branch of the capital structure literature are the articles by Grossman and Hart [1982], Hart and Moore [1995], Harris and Raviv [1990], Jensen [1986] and Stulz [1990].[41] Even though the number of these contributions is immense, literature has made very few attempts to provide a closed theory of controlling a self-interested management by the capital structure of the firm. While financing can theoretically be used to realign a divergence in interest between those providing a firm's funding and those who have discretionary power over the firm's assets, it is by no means an obvious candidate.

Existing theories have in common that management is pursuing its own goals at the expense of firm profit, which is usually the only thing that fund providers are interested in. But in that case, other incentive mechanisms, such as monetary compensation schemes based on verifiable output, could realign the diverging interests just as well. One has to ask the legitimate question why capital structure should be used to keep a check upon the management's misbehavior, when other devices are at hand. It seems much more appropriate to use direct contractual provisions well known from standard moral hazard problems.[42] From this perspective, models as presented in Grossman and Hart [1982], Hart and Moore [1995], Harris and Raviv [1990], Jensen [1986] and Stulz [1990], which just ignore standard monetary compensation schemes for the management, are not very convincing. Why should one want to withdraw funds in the form of a fixed debt obligation from management (as for example in Jensen [1986]) to prevent a profit decreasing use of these financial means, if one is able to achieve goal congruence by an appropriate wage schedule? The objection to financial structure as a disciplining device is based on the fact that most incentives one is able to provide by financial structure can be imitated by ordinary incentive schemes, which avoid the risk of bankruptcy. Therefore, it is not sufficient if financial structure can provide the same incentives as those

[41] Some of these theories have been reviewed in the literature survey of this book (see pp. 16 in Chapter 1).

[42] Grossman and Hart [1983], Holmström [1979], Hart and Holmström [1987] or Salanié [1997] provide the theoretical foundations for this. Furthermore see the book by Lazear [1995] for an extensive analysis of incentive contracts in employer-employee relationships.

other measures – it has to perform significantly better in some respects to become a viable disciplining tool.

Recent literature on financial structure has made progress in that direction. The reigning paradigm therein are incomplete contracts. This new approach, as represented by Aghion and Bolton [1989, 1922] or Dewatripont and Tirole [1994], shares the basic feature that some profit relevant contingencies have to be left out of the initial contract. This incompleteness of contracts is usually justified by the complexity of writing a complete contract. Aghion and Bolton [1992] explain financial structure as a device which determines who is allowed to make decisions in situations not covered in the initial contract. Within their framework, financial structure plays an important part even though monetary compensation is available. However in their model debt gains its relevance in a highly stylized manner of contingent control. Therefore it is contributing rather to the theory of control allocation than to the theory of capital structure itself.[43]

This Chapter will present a theory of capital structure as a disciplining device, in which debt does not gain its relevance by abstracting from all other tools available for realigning diverging interests. Our goal is to embed capital structure into a corporate governance framework, in which financing competes with the most obvious tool to mitigate conflicting interests, namely, monetary remuneration. The basis for our model is a simple principal-agent (investor-manager) world. We extend the standard model by two assumptions. As a first extension, the manager suffers a utility loss if the firm goes bankrupt under his management. In this, we follow Fama [1980, 291-2] or Firth [1995], who describe the cost of financial distress for managers' human capital. Secondly, we assume that the investor cannot punish her manager arbitrarily hard by means of the wage compensation schedule. She cannot do so, since her manager faces a wealth constraint which causes all monetary transfers from the investor to her agent to be non-negative. This results in a limitation of the feasible contract space for monetary compensation schedules. The minimum wage translates into a finite minimum utility level which can be imposed on the

[43] See the exposition of Aghion's and Bolton's model presented from page 28 on in Chapter 1.

manager. That is, our analysis takes place in a principal-agent framework with limited liability as presented by Sappington [1983] or Innes [1990].[44]

Within our setting, we are able to explain the coexistence of both incentive schemes, capital structure and standard monetary compensation. The general aim of our study is to show that combined incentives coming from a wage schedule *and* capital structure together may be cheaper than coming from the former device only. Debt financing can thus make sense even if the investor is wealthy enough to finance the project by herself.

Bensaid and de Bandt [1996] show that it may be optimal for an investment bank to apply a so-called "stop-loss rule" as a monitoring device for a trader facing limited liability. Their analysis is related to ours in the respect that a moral hazard problem between an investment bank and its trader is resolved by relying on an incentive scheme other than monetary compensation for reasons of limited liability. Grossman and Hart [1982] show that a manager can use debt as a precommitment device to indicate to the principal that he will act in the principal's interests. Their analysis – as ours – rests on the assumption that management is suffering a utility loss in financial distress.

We are closest in spirit to the paper by Schmidt [1997], who investigates the effects of product market competition on managerial incentive schemes. His work shows that increased product market competition can mitigate a principal-agent problem and benefit the principal by providing incentives to an agent, who is afraid of bankruptcy.

While the risk of financial distress is exogenously given in Schmidt's paper, it will be endogenously determined in our work by manipulating the capital structure in an optimal way. Our work is also related to Demougin and Fluet

[44] In Sappington [1983], the agent observes the state of the world before he takes his action, while Innes [1990] assumes that the agent does not know which state of the world has realized, when he is taking his action. Our model is similar to Innes [1990] in that the agent makes an ex-ante action choice. As our paper, Innes' work is located within a financial contracting world. In contrast to us, however, he is not concerned with an optimal choice of financing and the role of capital structure in providing incentives for the management.

[1997], who analyze the trade-off between monitoring and monetary incentives in a principal-agent relationship. We differ from them, in so far as we are concerned with the optimal mix of incentives stemming from capital structure and wages rather than from monitoring and incentive pay.

The remainder of this Chapter is structured as follows: The next section will lay out the model and comment on its basic assumptions. Section 3 will derive management's optimal incentive scheme as a combination of monetary wage payments and debt. In order to illustrate the key proposition, we develop a graphical tool to analyze the investor's decision problem concerning incentives provided to the subordinate. To gain some further insight, the graphical tool is applied to a numerical example in Section 5. A final Section summarizes our results and compares them to some empirical work and stylized facts concerning the corporate governance mechanisms of incentive pay and capital structure in different financial systems. All technical details and proofs can be found in the Appendix of this Chapter.

2.2 The Model

2.2.1 General Framework

An investor wants to set up a project, which requires expenditures of size $K > 0$. She cannot manage the firm by herself and has to delegate control over the firm's assets to a manager. The investor is concerned how her manager will act on her behalf. He can choose his effort from the set of effort levels $E = \{e_p, e_q\}$. The manager's disutility of choosing $e_n, n = p,q$, is given by $d(e_p)$ and $d(e_q)$ with $d(e_p) > d(e_q) \geq 0$. The choice of effort induces a probability distribution over a discrete random variable t which can take on realizations from the set $T = \{0,1\}$. p and q constitute probabilities in the following sense:

$$\Pr(t = 1, e = e_p) = p, \Pr(t = 0, e = e_p) = (1 - p)$$

and

$$\Pr(t = 1, e = e_q) = q, \Pr(t = 0, e = e_q) = (1 - q),$$

with $0<q<p<1$. t = 1 is a favorable event for the investor since it is affecting in a positive way the density from which the firm's gross profit is drawn. Let $f(x,t)$ be the density function underlying the firm's cash flow with

$$f(x,t)=t\cdot f^H(x)+(1-t)\cdot f^L(x),$$

where $f^H(x)$ and $f^L(x)$ are density functions over a given support $X=\{\underline{x},\bar{x}\}$. Assume that $0\le \underline{x}<K<\bar{x}<\infty$. The former density function $f^H(x)$, is assumed to dominate the latter $f^L(x)$, in the sense of first-order stochastic dominance, i.e.

$$\int_{\underline{x}}^{\hat{x}} f^H(x)dx \le \int_{\underline{x}}^{\hat{x}} f^L(x)dx \qquad \forall \hat{x}\in X$$

We furthermore require that $f^H(x)$ and $f^L(x)$ are continuous functions, which are continuously differentiable. By these assumptions, the two densities will intersect at least once on the open interval $(\underline{x},\bar{x})$, but we impose the assumption that they intersect exactly once. Denote this point of intersection by $\tilde{x}$. By first-order stochastic dominance we must have $f^H(x)-f^L(x)\le 0$ for $\underline{x}\le x\le \tilde{x}$ and $f^H(x)-f^L(x)\ge 0$ for $\tilde{x}<x\le \bar{x}$.

By exerting effort e_n, n = p, q, the manager in effect chooses a convex combination over the two specified density functions. In other words, his choice parametrizes a distribution function over final outcomes, where e_p induces a function, which dominates that induced by in the sense of first-order stochastic dominance. Furthermore assume that $q\cdot d(e_p)>p\cdot d(e_q)$.[45]

The manager's choice of e_p (e_q) will cause the firm's final profit to be drawn from the density function $f^H(x)$ with probability p (q), and from density $f^L(x)$ with probability $(1-p)$ $((1-q))$. In other words, if the manager is working hard

[45] This assumption is not necessary for the problem we are going to address. It will, however, rule out cases which are not interesting for our analysis here. we will come back to the role of this assumption later.

(chooses e_p), he puts more probability mass on the event that x is drawn from $f^H(x)$ rather than from $f^L(x)$.

One can think of this situation in the following way. The manager can work hard to implement a certain plan or business strategy, but for any effort choice e_n, $n = p, q$, he is only successful with probability n. In case of success, the firm's profit is drawn from the "favorable" density $f^H(x)$, while in case of failure it will be drawn from $f^L(x)$. Success or failure to implement the business strategy (i.e. the realization of the random variable t) is publicly observable and verifiable. The way our model is set up, the realization of t will not determine the firm's gross profit but only shift the odds in favor of or against the firm.[46]

The investor cannot observe her manager's effort choice, but she may employ monetary compensation to take care of the resulting moral hazard problem. Such a compensation scheme rewards the manager on the basis of his success or failure to implement the business strategy. Holmström's [1979] sufficient statistics result ensures that the investor can safely limit attention to a discrete compensation schedule contingent on the two outcomes $t = 1$ and $t = 0$. In other words, she can restrict herself to compensation schedules (w_H, w_L), which specify a monetary transfer from her to her subordinate contingent on the fact from which density function ($f^H(x)$ or $f^L(x)$) final outcome was drawn. Since the manager is wealth constrained, there is a non-negativity constraint on this monetary transfer, $w_i \geq 0, i = H, L$.

The investor is wealthy enough to finance the project on her own, but she may take on a bank credit, even though there is no primary need for that. If the firm defaults on its debt repayment, the manager is stigmatized for his future career as a manager and suffers a utility loss of $S > 0$, as mnemonic for stigma. S could either be a loss of reputation or material loss due to the fact that the managerial

---

[46] The reason why we choose this seemingly awkward modelling here is that we want to keep the analysis of the manager's compensation schedule as simple as possible, since the main focus is on capital structure. At the same time, we want to have a continuous set of possible profit levels in order to make the firm's financing decision interesting.

labor market now perceives the manager as a dull manager. This latter assumption is in the spirit of Fama [1980] and Gilson [1989, 1990]. The investor in our model decides how to finance the set-up cost at the beginning of the mutual relationship. She may go for full equity financing or even leverage the firm beyond a level of 100%. The deposit rate at which an individual can save, and at which the bank can refinance its loans is $(1+z)\geq 1$. Credit market is competitive, since it is made up of a large number of banks. Due to this competition among banks, opportunity cost of funds are just covered for any credit taken on. The interest rate (1 + *r*) at which a bank is willing to lend money will then adjust correspondingly. Debt levels *D* are chosen from the set $[0,\infty]$.[47]

The financing decision is simultaneously made with the decision on monetary compensation at date 1. The investor approaches the bank with this "package" at date 2, and this institution will decide whether it wants to grant credit at all. If the bank decides to do so, it will charge an interest rate which is leaving it at a zero profit in expected terms. The world ends if credit is refused. Provided that the bank has agreed to grant the loan, it is now up to the manager to make a decision at date 3. First of all, he must decide whether to sign the employment contract. Secondly, if he does sign the contract, he must decide what effort level to choose. Again, the world ends if the manager is not willing to sign the employment contract. Given that he was willing to work, *t* takes on its realization at date 4 which will determine whether the firm's gross payoff is drawn from $f^H(x)$ or $f^L(x)$. The random variable *x* immediately realizes after *t* has taken on its realization. Management will be paid the wage which has been laid down in the initial wage contract, and the firm will repay its debt or not depending on whether the generated cash flow is sufficient to service the outstanding obligations.

In case of bankruptcy, the bank takes over control and cashes in all the receipts from investment, while the investor does not receive any money out of the

---

[47] We will shortly see that the bank will refuse participation from a certain level on, and that there is an upper bound on debt levels that can be taken on.

project. For ease of exposition, assume that wages are not paid out of current receipts, but out of investor's private funds with the consequence that there is no risk of default on wage payments.[48] Furthermore, assume that the bank cannot seize the investor's private wealth if the firm defaults on its debt. In our simplified world, the firm is liquidated anyway at the end of the mutual relationship. For the manager, however, it is important whether the world ends with manager- or bank-control. He can avoid stigmatization only if the firm stays under his control during the whole time of the employment relationship. Figure 2.1 again demonstrates the timing of the model.

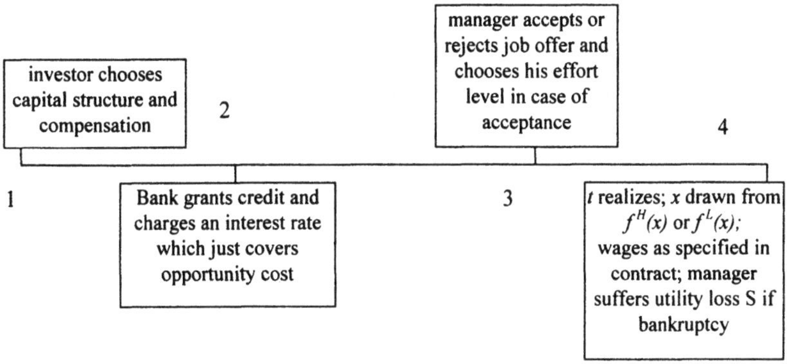

Figure 2.1: Timing of Events.

With respect to utility functions, assume that all players (investor, manager and bank) are risk-neutral. the investor and the bank are interested in (expected) monetary payoff only, while the manager is also interested in not being stigmatized. His expected utility is equal to the expected wage payment minus the utility loss S weighted with the probability of going bankrupt minus the disutility from work. The manager has a reservation utility of $\underline{u} = 0$ and will not accept to work under any combination of wage schedule and debt financing, which does not at least guarantee him a utility level of that height. Since the

[48] We will shortly see that the bank will refuse participation from a certain level on, and that there is an upper bound on debt levels that can be taken on.

wage payments must be non-negative, the manager's limited liability has the economic interpretation that he cannot be punished with a fine below his reservation utility. This will typically leave the manager with a positive rent and not hold him down to his reservation utility level.[49]

2.2.2 Some Remarks on the Driving Assumptions of the Analysis

Our model differs from standard principal-agent analysis by two assumptions. Firstly, not only does the manager derive utility out of monetary compensation, but he also suffers a loss in utility if a random variable takes on a realization below some level determined by debt financing. Secondly, the investor cannot punish her manager arbitrarily hard by means of the wage compensation schedule. These are the two assumptions which drive our results, and because of their importance we will comment on them before we start our analysis.

The first assumption is actually the most important one, which gives capital structure as an incentive device its meaning. There would be no reason at all to fall back on it for that purpose, if the manager did not have any interest in avoiding financial distress. The manager's utility loss could either be a damage to his professional reputation, a loss of firm specific investment in human capital, or finally it could stand for a concrete reduction in income, since managers of bankrupt firms may find it difficult to be placed into comparable top positions again. Theoretical and empirical underpinning for this assumption can be found in Fama [1980], Firth [1995] and Gilson [1989, 1990].[50]

---

[49] In fact the assumption $q \cdot d(e_p) > p \cdot d(e_q)$ is made to restrict attention to cases in which the manager is receiving a rent if the probability of financial distress is 0.

[50] Firth [1995 takes the view that the consequences of financial distress for management's firm specific investment into human capital play an important role for the firm's choice of financing. "Managers are likely to prefer moderate or low levels of corporate debt as it is in their self-interest to reduce the chances of corporate bankruptcy. The investment of human capital in the company they manage, together with the increased difficulty of finding new employment (enhanced because of their 'association' with a failed or poorly performing firm), will influence senior executives to make conservative business decisions and follow prudent financing policies." (Firth [1995, 167)

Gilson [1989], is giving a nice real world example, demonstrating that a firm's financial distress is indeed affecting its management's career path: "[Mr. Aweida] said he knew his

One could try to invalidate our model by proposing to set a firm internal minimum profit level in order to imitate external debt. The manager would be fired, if he failed to achieve this minimum profit level. Such an internal debt imitation could create the same incentives as bank credit, without incurring the risk of bankruptcy. However, we are convinced that a default on bank credit is fundamentally different from a default on an internally agreed-upon minimum profit level. The financial press is usually reporting on firms which have trouble in paying back their debt. It is doubtful whether the failure to achieve some internally specified profit level would attract any attention from outside. However, if banks are involved, the financial situation leaks out, at the latest, as soon as there is some discussion among banks how to settle some outstanding debt. This publicity will usually leave the financial community uncertain about the manager's skills and thus lead to consequences as described above.

Economic theory in the form of principal-agent analysis tells us that compensation schemes based on verifiable output do very well in keeping a self-interested management in check. And indeed, the existence of elaborated compensation contracts and bonus schemes for managers suggest that monetary compensation is playing a key role in aligning diverging interests. But literally any monetary incentives we observe in reality are carrots without sticks. While a principal can reward her agent with a positive sum of money, the lowest monetary punishment she can impose on her subordinate is a low positive amount or at the utmost an amount of 0. In other words, fines for bad performance are hardly observed in practice in an employer-employee relationship.

A direct theoretical consequence of restricting the set of available wage compensation contracts by non-negativity constraints is that the implementation of specific effort levels is becoming more expensive. Especially, high powered incentives are becoming more costly, since incentives at first mean rewards, not fines. We suggest that monetary compensation schedules do not perform very

---

days with Storage Technology were numbered once the company entered bankruptcy-law proceedings. 'Obviously you can't do anything right after that', he said. 'People have short memories.'" (WSJ, 1982, August 2, 20; quoted after Gilson [1989, 256])

well if the presence of a limited liability constraint causes that the investor cannot punish her manager arbitrarily hard by means of monetary compensation. In such a situation, it may become interesting for the investor to rely on capital structure as an additional incentive scheme.

2.3 Analysis of the Model

The investor is facing a classical principal-agent problem as described by Grossman and Hart [1983] or Holmström [1979]. She has to design an incentive scheme, comprising a monetary reward scheme and debt, which induces the manager to take the option most preferred by her, i.e. either e_p or e_q. The problem acquires interest only if she desires to implement e_p. This is the case since e_q – the least cost action – can simply be implemented by taking on no debt at all and by paying the manager a fixed wage equal to $\underline{u} + d(e_q)$, leaving him indifferent between accepting or rejecting the investor's job offer. Incentives are not necessary. In order to make the problem one of interest, we will therefore assume that she wants to implement high effort.[51] Since she cannot observe her manager's choice of effort, she must design incentives to stimulate voluntary effort on the manager's side. That is, her most preferred option must be the one which is maximizing his expected utility.

2.3.1 Bank Participation and Interest Rate *r(D)*

Let us take a look on debt and the interest rate first. The bank will receive an agreed-upon debt repayment $D \cdot (1 + r)$ or cash in the complete final profit, depending on whether the firm is in default or not. Assume that the bank can be sure of management choosing e_p. Now, to guarantee bank participation, the following must be true:

$$p \cdot \int_{\underline{x}}^{D\cdot(1+r)} x \cdot f^H(x)\,dx + (1-p) \cdot \int_{\underline{x}}^{D\cdot(1+r)} x \cdot f^L(x)\,dx$$

[51] In order to check whether this is indeed the case one will have to compare her expected payoff from implementation of e_p with that at e_q .

$$+ p \cdot D \cdot (1+r) \cdot \int_{D \cdot (1+r)}^{\bar{x}} x \cdot f^H(x)\, dx \qquad \text{(BP)}$$

$$+ (1-p) \cdot D \cdot (1+r) \cdot \int_{D \cdot (1+r)}^{\bar{x}} x \cdot f^L(x)\, dx \qquad \geq D \cdot (1+z),$$

i.e. the bank's expected payoff in taking part must exceed its refinancing cost of the loan. We will refer to this condition as the bank's participation constraint, (BP).

The firm may go bankrupt whether the manager was successful or not, in which case the bank becomes residual claimant of the firm (this is the first line). The agreed repayment is made if the firm is not in financial distress, which is what the second convex combination in line two and three states. The total sum must exceed the bank's cost of granting the loan D to the firm. Competition among banks will cause that (BP) is always binding for an arbitrary incentive scheme (w_H, w_L, D) that achieves implementation of e_p. To ensure this, the interest rate $(1 + r)$ must adjust accordingly.

Up to a debt level of $\underline{x}/(1 + z)$, debt is not risky, since even the lowest realization of x is sufficient to repay the outstanding debt obligation. As a consequence, any credit taken on up to this point will bear the interest rate $(1 + z)$, i.e. it will be paid off with the bank's refinancing cost. Above this level, debt becomes risky. Therefore, the bank will demand a compensation for the risk that the firm defaults on its debt, i.e. $(1 + r)$ must arise above $(1 + z)$.

The bank will never be prepared to grant a credit that requires a repayment $D \cdot (1 + r)$ in excess of $\bar{x}$. Even though the bank is then residual claimant for any realization of x, it will not accept such a deal, because the expected profits will not suffice to cover the cost of granting such a loan. The binding bank participation for a repayment at which the bank is the firm's residual claimant for all states of the world in X, determines an upper bound on credit to be taken on by the investor. The maximum debt the firm is willing to grant to the investor (given the manager' effort choice is fixed to e_p) is equal to the project's total expected payoff discounted by the refinancing rate. One can easily verify this by substituting $D \cdot (1 + r) = \bar{x}$ into the LHS of (BP). For convenience we will adopt the following definition.

Definition 1 Under the assumption that effort is exogenously fixed at e_p, the interval to which the investor's choice of debt is restricted according to the bank's participation constraint is specified by

$$\left[0, D^{Max}\right] = \left[0, \frac{p \cdot \int_{\underline{x}}^{\bar{x}} x \cdot f^H(x)dx + (1-p) \cdot \int_{\underline{x}}^{\bar{x}} x \cdot f^L(x)dx}{(1+z)}\right]$$

The interest rate *r(D)* will adjust to the point where the bank is left with a zero profit, i.e. r is implicitly determined by the bank's binding participation constraint. By the implicit function theorem, this implicit function *r(D)* here is continuous and has a continuous derivative r_D according to the following statement:

Proposition 1 Given the manager exerts effort e_p , the function r(D) is monotonically increasing in debt, D, from the interval $(0,D^{Max})$.

Proof: See Appendix. ■[52]

2.3.2 Investor's Payoff and Maximization Problem

Since investor and manager are risk neutral, an obvious solution seems to be that the manager should buy the firm from the investor to run it on his own accounts. This would eliminate the friction caused by unobservable effort. But the manager is completely penniless and so this solution is ruled out here. Due to his wealth restriction, he cannot compensate the investor ex-ante to transfer ownership to himself. We furthermore assume that such a transaction cannot be

[52] The reason to state this Proposition for the open interval has technical reasons – the prerequisites for applying the implicit function theorem are not satisfied at $D = 0$ and $D = D^{Max}$.

made by compensating the investor ex-post by promising expected cash flow to the investor accrued under the manager's sole ownership. For the remainds of this Chapter we rule out this so-called "selling-the-store-solution". Delegation of control to a second party is viewed as an inherent feature of the investment project. The fact that the manager cannot be punished arbitrarily hard by means of the monetary compensation scheme due to his wealth constraint nicely fits the assumption that he is completely penniless and thus cannot buy the firm in an ex-ante agreement.

As before, we fix the manager's effort at e_p. Then the investor's expected payoff (before paying wages but after debt repayment) from investment with a certain amount of debt D, requiring a repayment of $D \cdot (1 + r(D))$, is

$$p \cdot \int_{D\cdot(1+r(D))}^{\bar{x}} x \cdot f^H(x)dx + (1-p) \cdot \int_{D\cdot(1+r(D))}^{\bar{x}} x f^L(x)dx$$

$$-p \cdot D \cdot (1+r(D)) \cdot \int_{D\cdot(1+r(D))}^{\bar{x}} x \cdot f^H(x)dx$$

$$-(1-p) \cdot D \cdot (1+r(D)) \int_{D\cdot(1+r(D))}^{\bar{x}} x \cdot f^L(x)dx - (K-D) \cdot (1+z),$$

where the interest rate $r(D)$ is determined as derived in the appendix. The first convex combination is the investor's expected payoff contingent on the firm not going bankrupt, while the second convex combination is the expected debt repayment given that the firm is able to service outstanding debt. The final term captures that the investor has opportunity cost of $(1+z)$ on each Dollar she puts into the project. Remember that she could just as well deposit her funds with the bank to obtain a deposit rate of $(1+z)$. Since the bank's participation constraint is necessarily binding one can substitute $D \cdot (1 + z)$ from there into the above expression to obtain

$$p \cdot \int_{\underline{x}}^{\overline{x}} x \cdot f^H(x)dx + (1-p) \cdot \int_{\underline{x}}^{\overline{x}} x \cdot f^L(x)dx - K \cdot (1+z) \tag{2.1}$$

as the investor's expected payoff before wage payments, given the manager's effort level is exogenously fixed at e_p.

Debt does not enter this latter expression, and, at first, the insight of Modigliani and Miller [1958] that financing policy is inconsequential to the cash flow generated, seems to be rediscovered here. But this conclusion would be short-sighted, for the expression states that payoff *before* wage payments is unaffected by the financing decision. It therefore becomes clear from this expression that, if debt financing becomes relevant in our model, it must be through its influence on expected wage payments. We will find this insight confirmed by the investor's maximization problem. This problem is to implement effort e_p such that implementation costs (i.e. expected wage payments) are minimized.

In order to derive the optimal incentive scheme for implementation of e_p, we will rely on a tool which is quite frequently used in the framework of principal-agent problems, namely the so-called two step procedure (e.g. see Kreps [1990, pp. 586]). The idea of this procedure is first to specify a certain effort level from the set of available effort levels E and then to look for the cheapest way to implement this fixed effort level. This is done for each effort level in the set E. Given that the principal can find a way to implement any available effort level, a second step then proceeds to look for the specific effort level among all implementable ones which is maximizing the principal's expected payoff.

The application of this procedure is particularly easy here since the manager has only two effort levels to choose from. We have already mentioned that implementation of e_q is not very challenging, so that we will concentrate on implementation of e_p. We will have to ask ourselves later whether the investor will really find it worthwhile to implement e_p, but for the moment let us simply assume that this is the case. The determination of the interest rate *r(D)* in the following maximization problem is treated as if the bank could be sure that e_p is chosen by the manager. Of course, this choice must be incentive compatible. However this is required by one of the constraints under which maximization takes place. The maximization problem to find the optimal incentive scheme for implementation of e_p is then given through:

$$\max_{(w_H, w_L, D)} - p \cdot w_H - (1-p) \cdot w_L$$

s.t.

$$p \cdot w_H + (1-p) \cdot w_L - d(e_p) - S \cdot \left[p \cdot \int_{\underline{x}}^{D\cdot(1+r(D))} f^H(x)dx + (1-p) \cdot \int_{\underline{x}}^{D\cdot(1+r(D))} f^L(x)dx \right] \geq 0 \qquad \text{(PC)}$$

$$p \cdot w_H + (1-p) \cdot w_L - d(e_p) - S \cdot \left[p \cdot \int_{\underline{x}}^{D\cdot(1+r(D))} f^H(x)dx + (1-p) \cdot \int_{\underline{x}}^{D\cdot(1+r(D))} f^L(x)dx \right]$$

$$\geq \qquad \text{(IC)}$$

$$q \cdot w_H + (1-q) \cdot w_L - d(e_q) - S \cdot \left[p \cdot \int_{\underline{x}}^{D\cdot(1+r(D))} f^H(x)dx + (1-q) \cdot \int_{\underline{x}}^{D\cdot(1+r(D))} f^L(x)dx \right]$$

$$w_H \geq 0 \qquad \text{(LL-H)}$$

$$w_L \geq 0 \qquad \text{(LL-L)}$$

$$D^{Max} - D \geq 0 \qquad \text{(D-Max)}$$

The constraints of this problem deserve some comments. (PC) is the participation constraint, which assures that the manager is indeed willing to work for the investor and at least receives an expected payoff $\underline{u} = 0$ by accepting the terms of business. He will not accept any combination of wage schedule and debt financing, which does not at least guarantee him his reservation utility level. (IC) restricts incentive schemes to those which make it in the manager's own interest to pick e_p rather than e_q. Since contracts cannot contain a clause specifying the manager's action, the effort level which is to be implemented must maximize the manager's expected utility. The two constraints (LL-H) and (LL-L) are the non-negativity constraints on wage payments which we have discussed above. Finally, the constraint (D-Max) is a restriction on the maximum amount of debt, imposed on the investor by the bank's participation constraint. We do not introduce a non-negativity constraint for debt. It will become clear from the formal analysis why this is not necessary. Remember that we intend to model the incentive effects of bankruptcy here and that the firm can only go bankrupt for debts levels larger than zero. As we will shortly see the only advantage of debt financing is to make incentives cheaper. This cannot be achieved by taking on a negative credit (granting credit to some unmodelled agent). The Lagrangian for the problem and the corresponding first-order conditions are given in the Appendix to this Chapter.

In the following Section, we will now proceed to derive the incentive mix consisting of incentive pay and debt which achieves to implement e_p in the cheapest way. After the investor has found this incentive scheme, she can present it to the bank which will be willing to grant the desired debt level at an interest rate which is just covering its opportunity cost. The investor's expected gross payoff can then be stated as in expression (2.1) above. In order to obtain her payoff after wage payments one will have to subtract expected wage payments associated with the optimal incentive scheme from that expression.

2.3.3 The Optimal Incentive Scheme

Before we derive the incentive scheme which most cheaply achieves implementation of e_p, we will first clarify what role debt can play here. If the investor does not rely on debt financing at all, or takes on riskless debt only, the manager would not be threatened by the risk of bankruptcy. But then, any incentive to implement the more onerous action must origin from the – monetary compensation schedule.

The situation is different as soon as risky debt is taken on. In accordance with the assumptions on the density functions $f^H(x)$ and $f^L(x)$ as well as those on probabilities p and q, any debt taken on will induce a probability of bankruptcy, which is at least as high (but possibly higher) under low effort e_q as compared to high effort e_p. For that reason, a given debt level will constitute a greater risk of default for a lazy manager than for one who is working hard. In other words, there are incentives originating from debt. The *raison d'être* for debt financing is to provide part of the incentives for implementation of e_p through debt rather than to provide them purely through monetary remuneration.

In fact, the potential to lower expected implementation cost crucially hinges upon the assumption of limited liability. If the investor could punish her manager arbitrarily hard by means of the compensation schedule, there would be no role for debt financing at all. As we will show in the Appendix to this Chapter, this is the case since, in the absence of limited liability constraints, expected implementation cost are at a minimum level which cannot be undercut by relying on debt financing. Equivalently, debt financing would not have any effects on implementation cost, if management did not suffer a utility loss as a consequence of financial distress.

First of all, it is important to state that a combination of debt and wage incentive scheme exists which is able to implement e_p.

Proposition 2 There exists an optimal incentive scheme $\left(w_H^*, w_L^*, D^*\right)$, which achieves to implement the investor's most desired effort level e_p.

Proof: The objective function and the constraints containing the choice variables are continuous in the choice variables. A given debt level from the set of admissible debt levels $\left[0, D^{Max}\right]$ will induce a constraint set for w_H and w_L defined by (PC), (IC) and the two limited liability constraints which is non-empty by construction. This set is closed (all inequalities are weak) and bounded from below (by the non-negativity constraints on wage payments), but not from above. Fortunately, this unboundedness from above does not pose any problem to the existence of a wage schedule given D, since the objective function is strictly decreasing in w_H and w_L. Therefore, an optimal wage incentive scheme will necessarily exist for a given debt level from the specified interval. Since the set of admissible debt levels constitutes a closed and bounded set, there will exist a combination of wage incentive scheme and debt $\left(w_H^*, w_L^*, D^*\right)$, which maximizes the investor's payoff. ■

Proposition 3 The optimal incentive scheme $\left(w_H^*, w_L^*, D^*\right)$ is unique and characterized by

$$w_H^*\left(D^*\right)=\frac{1}{(p-q)}\cdot\left[d\left(e_p\right)-d\left(e_q\right)+S\cdot(p-q)\cdot\int_{\underline{x}}^{D^*\cdot(1+r(D^*))}\left(f^H(x)-f^L(x)\right)dx\right]$$

$$w_L^*\left(D^*\right)=0$$

as the optimal wage schedule and

$$D^*=\begin{cases} D^+ \; for \; \frac{1}{S}\cdot\frac{q\cdot d\left(e_p\right)-p\cdot d\left(e_q\right)}{(p-q)}\leq 1 \\ \hat{D} \quad otherwise \end{cases}$$

as the optimal debt level, with $D^+ and\ \hat{D}$ as debt levels from the interval $[0, D^{Max}]$ implicitly defined by

$$\frac{1}{S}\cdot\frac{q\cdot d\left(e_p\right)-p\cdot d\left(e_q\right)}{(p-q)}-\int_{\underline{x}}^{D^+\cdot\left(1+r\left(D^+\right)\right)} f^L(x)dx=0 \text{ and}$$

$$f^H\left(\hat{D}\cdot\left(1+r\left(\hat{D}\right)\right)\right)-f^L\left(\hat{D}\cdot\left(1+r\left(\hat{D}\right)\right)\right)=0 \text{ respectively.}$$[53]

Proof: See Appendix. ■

The investor will choose an optimal wage schedule which has a relatively simple structure, independent of what the optimal debt level turns out to be. She will always pay her manager a strictly positive wage in case of success, while he will receive a wage of zero if he fails to implement the business strategy. Punishment by means of the wage payment is as severe as it can be in this latter case. One can see this from the non-negativity constraint on the wage payment w_L, which is binding at the optimal solution. Relaxing this constraint will make the investor better off. We mentioned earlier that the restriction of wage contracts to non-negative transfers will make an implementation of e_p more costly. This is confirmed here.

One can generally state that debt complements the wage incentives in such a way that implementation cost of e_p are brought to a global minimum. How this minimization problem is solved deserves some further discussion. We will reformulate the problem into a minimization problem of expected wage payments, with debt as the only remaining choice variable to illustrate the results stated in Proposition 3.

In order to understand the investor's optimal choice of D, it is crucial to see that the participation constraint can be binding or slack at the optimal solution. The standard result of principal-agent theory without limited liability constraints is that the agent's participation constraints is binding.[54] The reasoning for that roughly runs as follows: Assume that the principal wants to implement an action which is not a least-cost action (i.e. her problem is not trivial) and that the (PC) is slack at the optimal solution. She can now lower the wage payments to her agent in each of the countably many and verifiable states on which wage payments are contingent by the same amount $\varepsilon > 0$ until (PC) becomes binding. This leaves the (IC) unaffected (all wage payments are lowered by the same

[53] D^+ may not exist, which is however just the case in which $\hat{D}$ is chosen.

[54] See for example Kreps [1988, 591] for a textbook exposition of this result.

amount), while it lowers expected wage payments. But then, the contract at which (PC) was slack cannot have been optimal in the first place. This argument does not work here, since wage payments cannot be lowered arbitrarily due to the non-negativity constraints on wage payments and as a result the participation constraint might be slack at the optimal solution.

The investor seeks to minimize the expected wage payments to her subordinate subject to the constraint that the manager is willing to accept the job offer and that he is working hard. These expected wage payments are given by

$$c^e(w_H, w_L) = p \cdot w_H + (1-p) \cdot w_L .$$

Let $\left(\left(w_H^*(D), w_L^*(D)\right)\right)$ be the tupel of wage payments which implements e_p subject to the constraint set induced by some admissible D at minimum expected cost. As we show in the Appendix to this Chapter, the optimal wage schedule at D^* must have the structure $\left(w_H^* > 0, w_L^* = 0\right)$. We can therefore restrict our search of optimal debt levels to those from a set $D^\#$, which are inducing wage contracts of that kind. Now, substituting $w_H(D)$ as specified in equation (2.19) and $w_L = 0$ into the expression for expected wage payments generates

$$c^e\left(\left(w_H^*(D), w_L^* = 0\right)\right) =$$

$$\frac{p}{(p-q)} \cdot \left[d(e_p) - d(e_q) + S \cdot (p-q) \cdot \int_{\underline{x}}^{D \cdot (1+r(D))} \left(f^H(x) - f^L(x)\right) dx \right]. \qquad (2.2)$$

The investor's task is now to minimize this latter expression by a diligent choice of debt from the intersection of the two sets $D^\#$ and $[0, D^{Max}]$.[55]

Let us turn fist to the case in which the participation constraint is slack. If this is the case at the optimal solution, the investor only cares about the incentive role

[55] It is straightforward to show that the intersection of those sets is non-empty and constitutes a closed and bounded set. Since these comments are only a different view on the investor's payoff maximization problem, we omit any proofs here.

of debt and not about the fact that debt financing is detrimental to the manager's utility level via the induced risk of bankruptcy. In order to minimize expected wage payments, the investor should leverage up the firm as much as she possibly can until she has reached the debt level $\hat{D}$ from which on additional debt is increasing w_H. From the first derivative of expression (2.2) with respect to D given by

$$\partial c^e / \partial D = p \cdot S \cdot \left(f^H(D \cdot (1 + r(D))) - f^L(D \cdot (1 + r(D)))\right) \cdot ((1 + r(D)) + D \cdot r_D),$$

it is obvious that debt financing can only benefit the investor as long as the density function f^H evaluated at the repayment due, $D \cdot (1 + r(D))$, is smaller than the density function f^L evaluated at this same level. The assumptions concerning the density functions above assure that the latter derivative is strictly decreasing in D until the total repayment due has reached the point of intersection $\tilde{x}$ between the two density functions. Since the two densities intersect in one point only on the interval $(\underline{x}, \bar{x})$ there is a unique optimal debt level for the case in which (PC) is slack. Additional debt can only benefit the investor as long as the marginal risk of bankruptcy given e_p is smaller than that at e_q.

In the second case, the participation constraint is binding at the optimal solution, which means that the investor must trade off the benefits of debt against its cost. The benefits are, of course, the incentives that origin from debt, while the cost are given by the threat of stigmatization induced. The optimal debt level D^+ will be determined by the binding participation and incentive constraints together with the expression of the optimal wage level w_H^*.

The investor tends to be (*ceteris paribus*) in a better position to extract all rents from her manager, the larger S, and the larger the difference in probabilities $p - q$. The optimal debt level given that (PC) can be brought to bind will decrease in the utility loss S, as one can see from Proposition 3.

As we have mentioned, one must now compare the investor's expected payoff from implementation of e_p to that associated with implementation of e_q. We assume that the model's parameters are such that the investor's most preferred effort level is indeed the one which is requiring to provide incentives to management.

2.4 Graphical Analysis

The investor's maximization problem can be analyzed in a (w_H, w_L)-diagram from which all the results concerning Proposition 3 can be received as well. We will first set up the prerequisites for this analysis, before we turn to a concrete numerical example in the next Section. Rearranging (PC) and (IC) brings us to

$$w_H \geq \frac{1}{p}\cdot\left[d\left(e_p\right)-d\left(e_q\right)\right]-\frac{(1-p)}{p}\cdot w_L + \frac{1}{p}\cdot S\cdot\left[p\cdot\int_{\underline{x}}^{D\cdot(1+r(D))} f^H(x)dx+(1-p)\cdot\int_{\underline{x}}^{D\cdot(1+r(D))} f^L(x)dx\right] \tag{2.3}$$

and

$$w_H \geq \frac{1}{(p-q)}\cdot\left[d\left(e_p\right)-d\left(e_q\right)\right]+w_L + S\int_{\underline{x}}^{D\cdot(1+r(D))}\left[f^H(x)-f^L(x)\right]dx. \tag{2.4}$$

The investor's objective function can be rearranged to obtain the level curve to a certain level of expected payoff π :

$$w_H = \frac{1}{p} \cdot [p \cdot \int_{\underline{x}}^{\bar{x}} x \cdot f^H(x) dx + (1-p) \cdot \int_{\underline{x}}^{\bar{x}} f^L(x) dx \qquad (2.5)$$

$$- K \cdot (1+z) - (1-p) \cdot w_L - \pi]$$

This latter expression can be used to draw isopayofflines into a (w_H, w_L)-diagram. Conditions (2.3) and (2.4) delineate a subset of the non-negative (w_H, w_L)-quadrant to which the maximization problem is restricted due to the two limited liability constraints. Depicting w_L on the abscissa and w_H on the ordinate, the set of wage contracts satisfying the participation constraint are those contracts above the line defined by a binding participation constraint, with a slope of $-(1-p)/p$. Similarly, the set of wage contracts satisfying the incentive constraint can be found above the line defined by the binding incentive constraint with the slope + 1.

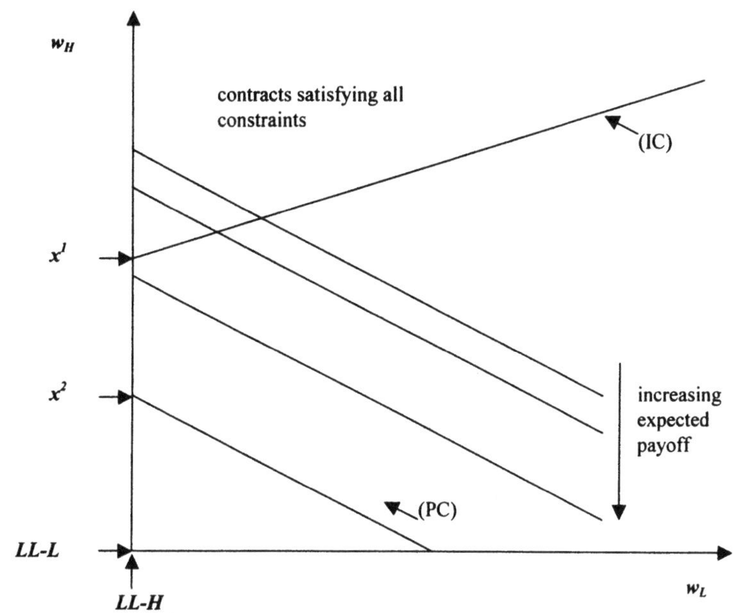

Figure 2.2: Constraint Set in the Absence of Debt.

As a point of reference, we have chosen the graph the situation in which the investor does not take on any risky debt at all. The manager is then not exposed to a risk of default and the graphical conditions for (PC) and (IC) become

$$w_H \geq \frac{1}{p}\cdot\left[d\left(e_p\right)-d\left(e_q\right)\right]-\frac{(1-p)}{p}\cdot w_L \text{ and } w_H \geq \frac{1}{(p-q)}\cdot\left[d\left(e_p\right)-d\left(e_q\right)\right]+w_L.$$

These conditions are (together with some isopayofflines) depicted in figure 2.2.

The intersection of (IC) and (PC) with the ordinate is referred to as x_1 and x_2 respectively. By the assumption $q\cdot d\left(e_p\right)>p\cdot d\left(e_q\right)$, the set to which the maximization takes place will be determined by the incentive constraint alone, i.e. the participation constraint is slack. Lower isopayofflines are associated with a higher expected payoff and one can easily see that the optimal wage schedule for this case will be given by

$$w_H=\frac{1}{(p-q)}\cdot\left[d\left(e_p\right)-d\left(e_q\right)\right] \text{ and } w_L=0.$$

The role of debt becomes especially clear, if we take a look on how the constraint set is altered by taking on risky debt. Remember that the bank will participate for debt levels in $[0, D^{Max}]$, but that debt becomes risky only above al level of $\underline{x}/(1+z)$. Taking on risky debt will shift the participation and the incentive constraint in the following way: (PC) is shifted outwards in the (w_H, w_L)-diagram, as risky debt is successively increased. In contrast to that, (IC) will shift towards the origin of the (w_H, w_L)-diagram up to a debt level $\hat{D}$ as defined above in Proposition 3. Beyond that debt level, the incentive constraint will start to shift outwards again. Looking at the constraints shows why this is the case. Financing the project partially by risky debt will add a positive number to the RHS of expression (2.3), which means that the corresponding line is shifted away from the origin. By the assumption of first-order stochastic dominance, increasing risky debt means to add a negative number to the RHS of (2.4) as long as the repayment due, $D \cdot (1 + r(D))$, is below $\hat{x}$. Accordingly, the corresponding line in a (w_H, w_L)-diagram will shift towards the origins as long as debt does not exceed this critical level. Increasing debt beyond that point will start to shift the incentive constraint in the opposite direction again.

It becomes obvious from how the constraint set is shifting that at $D = 0$ the investor can decrease expected wage payments by taking on risky debt thus shifting (IC) downwards. As the model is set-up, the manager will necessarily receive a rent in the absence of debt financing. Whether the investor is successful in extracting this rent from her subordinate by taking on debt depends on the model's special parameters, which finally determine whether the (PC) can be brought to bind or not.

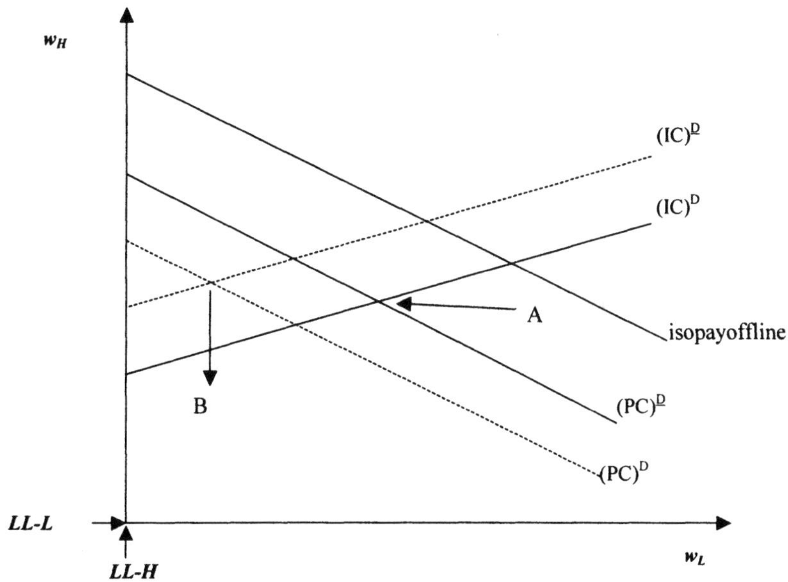

Figure 2.3: Constraint Shift Induced by a Change of D.

The optimal wage schedule must have the structure $w_H > 0$ and $w_L = 0$ in the absence of debt, but what about the wage schedule at the optimal debt level D^*, which could theoretically cause both wage payments to become strictly positive? Figure 2.3 demonstrates why this cannot be the case. Assume that (PC) and (IC) induced by some $\overline{D}$ intersect in a point A for which $w_H > 0$ and

$w_L > 0$ as depicted in figure 2.3. Such a situation can lead to a multiplicity of optimal wage contracts given *D*, since the investor's isopayoffline has the same slope as the manager's participation constraint. In fact, the only way that a multiplicity of solutions can come about is that – at the optimal solution – the level curve of the objective function is parallel to a segment of the set of feasible and incentive compatible contracts as defined by the constraints induced by the optimal *D*.

Yet, it is impossible that the isopayoffline coincides with the constraint set in more than one point for the following reason. Risky debt can be decreased to $\underline{D}$, shifting the (PC) and (IC) in such a way that they are intersecting in point *B*. Now, the investor can reach an isopayoffline which is closer to the origin. This argument can, however, be used until the point of intersection lies on the ordinate, which is implying $w_H > 0$ and $w_L = 0$. Thus, even though the objective function is linear in both choice variables, we obtain a unique incentive scheme $\left(w_H^*, w_L^*, D^*\right)$, as has been replicated by the graphical argument here.

To show our model at work, we are now going to present a numerical example, which we will analyze by applying the tool just developed.

2.5 A Numerical Example

Imagine that the investment cost *K* are given by *K* = 0.4, while the manager's effort levels e_p and e_q cause a disutility of $d(e_p) = 0.1$ and $d(e_q) = 0$ respectively. Let the probabilities *b* and *q* be given by 0.9 and 0.5. The choice of effort induces a density function $f(x,e_n)$ over the set of outcomes *X* given through [0,1]. The two density functions f^H and f^L, which constitute the density induced by a specific e_n

$$f(x,e_n) = n \cdot f^H(x) + (1-n) \cdot f^L(x), \qquad e_n \in \{e_{0.9}, e_{0.5}\}$$

shall be given by

$$f^H(x) = 2 \cdot x \text{ and } f^L(x) = 2 - 2 \cdot x .$$

Note that a probability distribution induced by $e_{0.9}$ is then dominating the one induced by $e_{0.5}$ in the sense of first-order stochastic dominance as required by the assumptions. Furthermore, let the manager's utility loss in case of financial distress be given by $S = 25/72$, while his reservation utility is given by $\underline{u} = 0$. The bank's refinancing rate $(1 + z)$ is 1, i.e. $z = 0$.

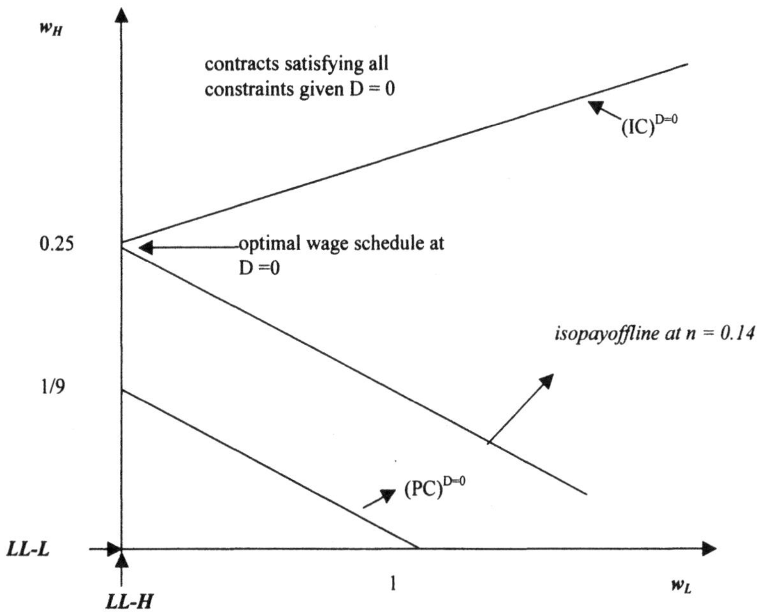

Figure 2.4: Optimal Wage Schedule at D = 0.

From the specified parameters follows that the investor can take on a maximum debt D^{Max} of $0.7\overline{6}$, which is the project's expected gross return. Debt becomes risky as soon as it is taken on since the lowest realization in X is 0. The two density function intersect at $\tilde{x} = 0.5$, from which follows that the investor will never take on debt requiring a repayment beyond 0.5, even though the bank would be willing to grant such credit. With the parameters given, the participation constraint and the incentive constraint in their graphical representation turn out to be

$w_H \geq$

$$\frac{1}{0.9}\cdot\left(0.1+\frac{25}{72}\cdot\left[0.9\cdot\int_0^{D\cdot(1+r(D))}2\cdot x dx+0.1\cdot\int_0^{D\cdot(1+r(D))}(2-2\cdot x)dx\right]\right)-\frac{1-0.9}{0.9}$$

and

$$w_H \geq \frac{0.1}{0.9-0.5}+\frac{25}{72}\cdot\left[\int_0^{D\cdot(1+r(D))}(4x-2)dx\right]+w_L.$$

The equation for the investor's isopayoffline is given by

$$w_H = \frac{1}{0.9}\cdot\left[0.3\overline{6}-\pi\right]-\frac{1-0.9}{0.9}\cdot w_L.$$

At a debt level of 0, we can infer from figure 2.4 that the optimal wage schedule is $w_H = 0.25$ and $w_L = 0$, leaving the investor with an expected payoff of approximately 0.14. Even though the manager has a reservation utility of $\underline{u} = 0$, he is receiving a payoff of $p\cdot 0.25 - d(e_{0.9}) = 0.9\cdot 0.25 - 0.1 = 0.125$ in this situation. Clearly, the investor can benefit by taking on risky debt, trying to extract some of the manager's rent. The condition which has to be satisfied to obtain a binding (PC) through an increase of debt is

$$\frac{1}{S}\cdot\frac{q\cdot d(e_p)-p\cdot d(e_q)}{(p-q)}\leq 1,$$

which holds here, since

$$\frac{72}{25}\cdot\frac{0.5\cdot 0.1}{(0.9-0.5)}=0.36<1$$

In other words, the investor can extract all rents from the manager and the (PC) will be binding at the optimal solution. The optimal repayment is characterized by the following condition

$$F^L(D\cdot(1+r(D)))=0.36,$$

which for our specified density function becomes

$$2\cdot D\cdot(1+r(D))-[D\cdot(1+r(D))]^2-0.36=0.$$

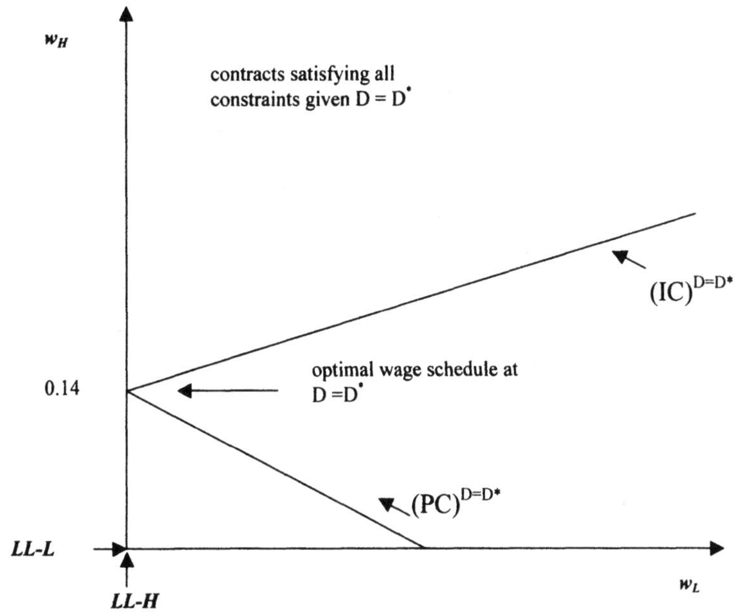

Figure 2.5: Optimal Wage Schedule at D = D*.

The corresponding quadratic has two solutions $D\cdot(1+r(D))$, namely 1.8 and 0.2, of which only the latter one is relevant for us here.

From the bank's binding participation constraint and the fact that z = 0, we obtain that the optimal debt level D^* is approximately 0.19, while the interest rate (1 + r) charged for this credit is approximately (1 ü 0.05). She should therefore finance approximately 50% of the project's set-up cost by debt. The manager's optimal wage, which goes together with the optimal repayment of 0.2, is

$$w_H = 0.25 + \frac{25}{72} \cdot \left[\int_0^{0.2} (4x-2)dx \right] \approx 0.14 .$$

By taking on debt, expected wage payments decrease from $0.9 \cdot 0.25 = 0.225$ to a level of $0.9\ 0.14 = 0.126$, i.e. the investor can save expected wage payments of something around 0.1 by adjusting her firm's leverage to the optimal level. At this optimal solution, the manager's rent has melted down to zero. The example just given demonstrates the case in which the optimal debt level is characterized by D^+ in the proposition, i.e. at the optimal solution the investor achieves to bring her employee down to his reservation utility. Figure 2.5 is depicting the constraint set for this situation and the isopayoffline to the expected payoff level $\pi = 0.24$, which is generated at the investor's optimal choice. It remains to compare the expected payoff from implementation of $e_{0.9}$ to the one associated with implementation of $e_{0.5}$. Even though implementation of low effort could be achieved at a flat wage payment of 0, the investor will choose to induce high effort as one can easily verify.

2.6 Conclusion

It has been argued here that capital structure can indeed have an incentive function in the moral hazard problem originating from the separation of ownership and control. The main contribution of our work is that, in contrast to many other agency-theoretic contributions, we do not gain our results by abstracting from the most obvious tool to regain goal congruence (monetary compensation). We rather show that combined incentives stemming from both devices can be beneficial to an investor. If a wealth restriction prevents the investor from punishing her manager arbitrarily hard by means of the compensation schedule, it may be valuable to rely on both mechanisms. By doing so, the investor can cut back on expected wage payments to her manager by providing incentives through financial structure. Debt financing is found to be of value, even though the investor has enough funds to finance the project by herself.

Apart from complementing the arguments of Grossman and Hart [1982], Hart and Moore [1995] and other representatives of the agency view on capital structure, there is also a corporate governance dimension to our contribution. The interplay of the two corporate governance mechanisms of incentive pay and capital structure is at the heart of our analysis. While the existing corporate governance literature (e.g. see Shleifer and Vishny [1997]) has a lot to say about each of the mechanisms in isolation, it is rather silent on how they might be intertwined. Our model is contributing to this question, in the sense that it is providing a basis for the firm's decision to choose a mix of the two incentive schemes. From this viewpoint our model is endogenizing the origins of incentives provided.

There has been much discussion on the effectiveness of top-management incentive compensation in increasing firm performance. Examples for this empirical literature are Agrawal and Knoeber [1996], Garvey, McCorry and Swan [1996], Jensen and Murphy [1990] and Murphy [1985]. Evidence from these studies is conflicting. Though almost every study points out a statistically significant relationship between top-management's incentive pay and firm performance, they are not unanimous on how strong this relationship is. Jensen and Murphy [1990], for example, conclude that the link between performance and pay is rather low, and Murphy [1985] finds that pay is approximately three times more sensible to firm size than to firm performance.[56] While it seems not clear how valuable high-powered monetary incentives really are for shareholders, empirical observations suggest that the importance of incentive pay differs very much across countries with different financial systems.

As a stylized fact, high powered monetary incentives are widespread in countries belonging to the Anglo-Saxon type of financial system, while bonus schemes and stock-option plans seem to be less common in countries belonging

[56] This latter finding is suggesting that there might be something to Jensen's [1986] free cash flow hypothesis, and the argument that management is very concerned with profit depressing firm growth rather than paying out funds as dividends. These empirical findings do of course not explain why the monetary incentive schemes are not sharpened as a result.

to the bank-based system.[57] At the same time, firms in the former financial system tend to rely much less on debt financing, when compared to those in the latter countries, where banks are playing an important role in the provision of funds for investment. It is too daring to claim that our theory is explaining these stylized facts, but we want to be careful about that and state that empirical facts are at least consistent with our theory that debt can substitute for monetary incentives.[58] Given that a fixed dose of incentives is to be provided, a firm must choose a mix of monetary incentives and debt. Using our theory, one would argue that firms in the UK and the US do rely more heavily on success dependent wages, while firms in Japan and Germany provide a larger portion of incentives by means of debt.

2.7 Appendix

2.7.1 Interest Rate Behavior in Debt

For all of what follows assume that the manager's effort is exogenously fixed at e_p. The bank will be prepared to grant any loans up to the level of $\underline{x}/(1+z)$ at an interest rate of $(1 + z)$ as one can easily see from the bank's binding participation constraint (BP) at such debt levels. Above this critical level up to D^{Max}, the bank will still be prepared to grant credit, but debt becomes risky and the interest rate $(1 + r)$ must rise above $(1 + z)$ to compensate the bank for the risk of default. In this range, the interest rate $r(D)$ which the bank demands for risky debt, is implicitly determined by the bank's binding participation constraint. We write this latter expression as

$$\Phi(D,r) = p \cdot \int_{\underline{x}}^{D\cdot(1+r)} x \cdot f^H(x)dx + (1-p) \cdot \int_{\underline{x}}^{D\cdot(1+r)} x \cdot f^L(x)dx$$

[57] See Kaplan [1994] for a comparison of executive compensation schemes in Japan and the US.

[58] John and John [1993] provide a different explanation of why higher debt financing might be associated with low-powered executive compensation. In contrast to our model, they do not

$$+ p \cdot D \cdot (1+r) \cdot \int_{D \cdot (1+r)}^{\bar{x}} x \cdot f^H(x) dx$$

$$+ (1+p) \cdot D \cdot (1+r) \cdot \int_{D \cdot (1+r)}^{\bar{x}} x \cdot f^L(x) dx - D \cdot (1+z) = 0 .$$

This function has continuous partial derivatives $\partial\Phi / \partial D$, and $\partial\Phi / \partial r$ and at any (*D*, *r*) with $D \in \left(0, D^{Max}\right)$ satisfying the equation, $\partial\Phi / \partial r$ is non-zero. calculating the partials brings us to

$$\partial\Phi / \partial D =$$

$$p \cdot (1+r) \cdot \int_{D \cdot (1+r)}^{\bar{x}} x \cdot f^H(x) dx$$

$$+ (1+p) \cdot (1+r) \cdot \int_{D \cdot (1+r)}^{\bar{x}} x \cdot f^L(x) dx - (1-z),$$

which must be smaller than zero as one can see by the bank's binding participation constraint and

$$\partial\Phi / \partial D =$$

$$p \cdot D \cdot \int_{D \cdot (1+r)}^{\bar{x}} x \cdot f^H(x) dx$$

---

adopt a governance view on the firm's financing decision, i.e. debt does not play a role of an incentive device in their framework.

$$+(1-p)\cdot D\cdot \int_{D\cdot(1+r)}^{\bar{x}} x\cdot f^{L}(x)dx,$$

which must necessarily be greater than zero. By the implicit function theorem this generates

$$r_D = -\frac{p\cdot(1+r)\cdot \int_{D\cdot(1+r)}^{\bar{x}} x\cdot f^{H}(x)dx+(1-p)\cdot D\cdot \int_{D\cdot(1+r)}^{\bar{x}} x\cdot f^{L}(x)dx}{p\cdot D\cdot \int_{D\cdot(1+r)}^{\bar{x}} x\cdot f^{H}(x)dx+(1-p)\cdot D\cdot \int_{D\cdot(1+r)}^{\bar{x}} x\cdot f^{L}(x)dx}.$$

This last expression is greater than zero. Thus it follows that the interest rate *r(D)* is a monotonically increasing function in debt levels from $(0,D^{Max})$. ■

2.7.2 Lagrangian and Kuhn-Tucker Conditions for the Investor's Maximization Problem

The Lagrangian for the investor's problem is

$$L(w_H, w_L, D; \lambda_{PC}, \lambda_{IC}, \lambda_{LL-L}, \lambda_{LL-H}, \lambda_D)=$$

$$-p\cdot w_H-(1-p)\cdot w_L$$

$$+\lambda_{PC}\cdot\lfloor p\cdot w_H+(1-p)\cdot w_L-d(e_p)\rfloor$$

$$-S\cdot\left[p\cdot \int_{\underline{x}}^{D\cdot(1+r(D))} f^{H}(x)dx+(1-p)\cdot \int_{\underline{x}}^{D\cdot(1+r(D))} f^{L}(x)dx\right]]$$

$$+\lambda_{IC}\cdot[(p-q)\cdot w_H-(p-q)\cdot w_L-d(e_p)+d(e_q)$$

$$-S\cdot(p-q)\cdot\left[\int_{\underline{x}}^{D\cdot(1+r(D))}\left[f^H(x)-f^L(x)\right]dx\right]\Bigg]$$

$$+\lambda_{LL-L}\cdot[w_L]$$

$$+\lambda_{LL-H}\cdot[w_H]$$

$$+\lambda_D\cdot[D^{Max}-D],$$

where $\lambda_{PC},\lambda_{IC},\lambda_{LL-L},\lambda_{LL-H}$ and λ_D are the respective multipliers on the constraints as specified by the indices.

A solution (if there is existing one) to the problem $\left(w_H^*,w_L^*,D^*\right)$ must satisfy the following conditions[59]

$$\frac{\partial L}{\partial w_H}=-p+p\cdot\lambda_{PC}+(p-q)\cdot\lambda_{IC}+\lambda_{LL-H}=0 \tag{2.6}$$

$$\frac{\partial L}{\partial w_L}=-(1-p)+(1-p)\cdot\lambda_{PC}-(p-q)\cdot\lambda_{IC}+\lambda_{LL-L}=0 \tag{2.7}$$

$$\frac{\partial L}{\partial D}=+\lambda_{PC}\cdot S\cdot\left[p\cdot f^H(D\cdot(1+r))+(1-p)\cdot f^L(D\cdot(1+r))\right]\cdot[(1+r)+D\cdot r_D]$$

$$+\lambda_{IC}\cdot S\cdot(p-q)\cdot[f^H(D\cdot(1+r))-f^L(D\cdot(1+r))]\cdot[(1+r)+D\cdot r_D] \tag{2.8}$$

$$+\lambda_D=0$$

59 For ease of notation, we write $(1+r)$ rather than $(1+r(D))$ here.

$$\lambda_{PC} \cdot [p \cdot w_H + (1-p) \cdot w_L - d(e_p) - S \cdot \left[p \cdot \int_{\underline{x}}^{D\cdot(1+r)} f^H(x)dx + (1-p) \cdot \int_{\underline{x}}^{D\cdot(1+r)} f^L(x)dx \right]] = 0 \tag{2.9}$$

$$\lambda_{IC} \cdot [(p-q) \cdot w_H - (p-q) \cdot w_L - d(e_p) + d(e_q) - S \cdot (p-q) \cdot \left[\int_{\underline{x}}^{D\cdot(1+r)} \left[f^H(x) - f^L(x) \right] dx \right]] = 0 \tag{2.10}$$

$$\lambda_{LL-H} \cdot [w_H] = 0 \tag{2.11}$$

$$\lambda_{LL-L} \cdot [w_L] = 0 \tag{2.12}$$

$$\lambda_D \cdot [D^{Max} - D] = 0 \tag{2.13}$$

$$[p \cdot w_H + (1-p) \cdot w_L - d(e_p)] - S \cdot \left[p \cdot \int_{\underline{x}}^{D\cdot(1+r)} f^H(x)dx + (1-p) \cdot \int_{\underline{x}}^{D\cdot(1+r)} f^L(x)dx \right]] \geq 0 \tag{2.14}$$

$$[[(p-q) \cdot w_H - (p-q) \cdot w_L - d(e_p) + d(e_q)]$$

$$-S\cdot(p-q)\cdot\left[\int_{\underline{x}}^{D\cdot(1+r)}\left[f^{H}(x)-f^{L}(x)\right]dx\right]\geq 0 \tag{2.15}$$

$$w_H, w_L \geq 0 \tag{2.16}$$

$$[D^{Max}-D]\geq 0 \tag{2.17}$$

$$\lambda_{PC}, \lambda_{IC}, \lambda_{LL-L}, \lambda_{LL-H}, \lambda_D \geq 0 \tag{2.18}$$

2.7.3 Uniqueness of the Optimal Incentive Scheme

At an optimal solution, there are four possible combinations of multipliers on limited liability constraints, which we will name as follows:

	λ_{LL-L}	λ_{LL-H}
i)	$=0$	>0
ii)	>0	>0
iii)	$=0$	$=0$
iv)	>0	$=0$.

Each of the four possible cases shall now be analyzed.

Case i): It can be easily shown that $\lambda_{LL-L}=0, \lambda_{LL-H}>0$ is only compatible with conditions (2.6) and (2.7) for the following combinations of multipliers on (PC) and (IC): $\lambda_{PC}>0$ and $\lambda_{IC}>0$. Since (PC) and (IC) must be strictly binding expressions, (2.14) and (2.15) can be set equal. Making use of our knowledge that $w_H = 0$, this is resulting in a contradiction and therefore case i) $\lambda_{LL-L}=0$ and $\lambda_{LL-H}>0$ cannot prevail at the optimal solution.

Case ii): This case implies that both wage payments are 0, which violates the participation constraint and is therefore impossible.

Case iii): Applying the assumptions on multipliers in this case to expressions (2.6) and (2.7) generates

$$-p+p\cdot\lambda_{PC}+(p-q)\cdot\lambda_{IC}=0$$

and

$$-(1-p)+(1-p)\cdot\lambda_{PC}-(p-q)\cdot\lambda_{IC}=0$$

It follows from these equations that $\lambda_{PC}=1$ and $\lambda_{IC}=0$. $\lambda_{PC}=1$ implies that the inequality in inequality (2.14) can be replaced by an equality sign. Plugging this result into inequality (2.15) implies that the LHS of inequality (2.15) must be negative, which must not be the case here. Thus we can rule out case iii).

Case iv): This case cannot be brought to a contradiction and thus if there is existing a solution the optimal wage schedule must have this case as its basis. By conditions (2.6) and (2.7), (IC) must necessarily be binding in case iv), but (PC) may either be binding or slack, such that we are left with two possible combinations of multipliers $\lambda_{PC},\lambda_{IC},\lambda_{LL-L}$ and λ_{LL-H} that can possibly prevail at an optimal solution

$$\lambda_{PC}=0,\lambda_{IC}>0,\lambda_{LL-L}>0,\lambda_{LL-H}=0$$

and

$$\lambda_{PC}>0,\lambda_{IC}>0,\lambda_{LL-L}>0,\lambda_{LL-H}=0.$$

Because of the binding constraint on the low wage payment, it must be the case that $w_L = 0$. Furthermore, it follows from the binding incentive constraint that

$$w_H=\frac{1}{(p-q)}\cdot\left[d(e_p)-d(e_q)+S\cdot(p-q)\cdot\int\limits_{\underline{x}}^{D\cdot(1+r(D))}\left[f^H(x)-f^L(x)\right]dx\right]. \tag{2.19}$$

This expression still depends on the choice of D, which shall be analyzed now.

Debt Level

Claim: The constraint on maximum debt (D-Max) cannot be binding at the optimal solution.

Proof: Suppose it was. The investor would then choose D^{Max} characterized by $D^{Max} \cdot \left(1 + r\left(D^{Max}\right)\right) = \bar{x}$. We have shown above that the optimal wage schedule must have the structure $w_H > 0, w_L = 0$. By the assumption that D^{Max} is part of an optimal solution, the corresponding wage schedule $\left(w_H\left(D^{Max}\right), w_L = 0\right)$ must satisfy (IC) and (PC) as given through expressions (2.14) and (2.15). Now imagine that the investor decreases debt financing to a level D' associated with a repayment of $\tilde{x} < D' \cdot (1 + r(D')) < \bar{x}$, with $\tilde{x}$ as the unique point of intersection between the two densities in $(\underline{x}, \bar{x})$. By first-order stochastic dominance of $f^H(x)$ over $f^L(x)$, if a wage schedule $\left(w_H\left(D^{Max}\right), w_L = 0\right)$ is satisfying the constraints, so will $(w_H(D'), w_L = 0)$, as one can easily verify by comparing (PC) and (IC) for the case of D^{Max}, with (PC) and (IC) induced by D'. But then, the investor can lower expected wage payments from $p \cdot w_H\left(D^{Max}\right)$ to $p \cdot w_H(D')$, which means that the debt of D^{Max} cannot have been optimal. Thus constraint (D-Max) will not be active at the optimal solution. ∎

$\lambda_{PC} = 0$ as well as $\lambda_{PC} > 0$ is compatible with the system of equations written down above. We will now analyze each of two possible cases for λ_{PC} in turn.

i) $\lambda_{PC} = 0$: It follows from (2.8) that this can only be the case if we have

$$\lambda_{IC} \cdot [f^H(D \cdot (1 + r(D))) - f^L(D \cdot (1 + r(D)))] \cdot [(1 + r) + D \cdot r_D] = 0.$$

From the fact that $\lambda_{IC} > 0$ it follows that debt must be increased to the point at which the two density functions intersect, i.e. the optimal debt level $\hat{D}$ is implicitly characterized by $f^H\left(\hat{D} \cdot (1 + r(D))\right) - f^L\left(\hat{D} \cdot (1 + r(D))\right) = 0$.The economic interpretation of this critical debt level is that the marginal risk of bankruptcy is equal for each of the manager's two available actions.

By the optimal wage schedule, the expected wage payments are given by $p \cdot w_H$, which is – by first-order stochastic dominance of $f^H(x)$ over $f^L(x)$ – decreasing in E as long as $D \leq \hat{D}$. The investor should exploit this relationship and increase debt as long as it can help to cut back on expected wage payments. Beyond that threshold, debt will start to increase the optimal wage payment, which is why the investor will never choose any debt financing above the critical level of $\hat{D}$. Economically, the optimal debt level given that the participation constraint is slack can be interpreted as follows: The investor should increase the firm's debt financing up to the point at which additional debt cannot lower the expected wage payments anymore.

ii) $\lambda_{PC} = 0$: Participation constraint and incentive constraint are binding, i.e.

$$p \cdot w_H - d(e_p) - S \cdot \left[p \cdot \int_{\underline{x}}^{D \cdot (1+r(D))} f^H(x)dx + (1-p) \cdot \int_{\underline{x}}^{D \cdot (1+r(D))} f^L(x)\,dx \right] = 0$$

and

$$(p-q) \cdot w_H - d(e_p) + d(e_q) - S \cdot (p-q) \cdot \left[\int_{\underline{x}}^{D \cdot (1+r(D))} \left[f^H(x) - f^L(x) \right] dx \right] = 0.$$

From these two equations we obtain that

$$q \cdot w_H - d(e_q) - S \cdot \left[q \cdot \int_{\underline{x}}^{D \cdot (1+r(D))} f^H(x)dx + (1-q) \cdot \int_{\underline{x}}^{D \cdot (1+r(D))} f^L(x)\,dx \right] = 0$$

must be the case. Substituting the expression for w_H into this latter equation yields

$$\frac{q \cdot d(e_p) - p \cdot d(e_q)}{(p-q)} - S \cdot \int_{\underline{x}}^{D \cdot (1+r(D^+))} f^L(x)dx = 0.$$

From this expression one can read off the optimal debt level, supporting these circumstances D^+, which is implicitly defined by

$$\frac{1}{S}\cdot\frac{q\cdot d(e_p)-p\cdot d(e_q)}{(p-q)}-\int_{\underline{x}}^{D\cdot(1+r(D))} f^L(x)dx=0.$$

In order to find ourselves in this case, the exogenously given parameters must of course be such that

$$\frac{1}{S}\cdot\frac{q\cdot d(e_p)-p\cdot d(e_q)}{(p-q)}\leq 1.$$

The latter qualification decides whether the investor is able to hold the manager down to his reservation utility, or whether he is receiving a rent from his job. If it is not satisfied, (PC) cannot be binding and by our existence proof, we must therefore be in the case in which (PC) is slack.

This completes the proof of Proposition 3. ■

Chapter 3

Capital Structure and the Corporate Governance Role of Banks

3.1 Introduction

Recent years have witnessed an ever growing interest in firms' financing decisions related to the financial system in which firms are operating in (see e.g. Hellwig [1991] and Mayer [1988, 1990, 1998]). Most researchers and applied economists will easily accept the statement that the financial system of a country, with its special legal provisions and institutional peculiarities, has a large impact on the financial decision of a company, but opinions on how this decision is affected by various factors differ widely. At first glance, the observed systems as epitomized by the UK and the US on the one side (market-based system) and Japan and Germany on the other side (bank-based system) are different in their relative importance of financial institutions for the provision of financial means to companies.[60] But the differences go far beyond this empirical observation in that disparate financing patterns are only the consequence of more fundamental dissimilarities of the two systems.

Although it is generally accepted that banks play a prominent role in many economies, theoretical corporate finance literature has not yet given this fact its due attention. Mayer [1987, 470] notes that existing informational theories of capital structure are not likely to provide any satisfactory explanation for the firm's financing decision, as long as they neglect the role of financial

---

[60] See Chapter 1 for an exposition of both systems.

institutions. In the verbally oriented corporate governance literature, banks are commonly attributed a role as corporate monitors who seek to ensure that firm management is performing its task in the interest of owners.[61] There are also several detailed empirical studies on this role of banks (e.g. Edwards and Fischer [1994], Hoshi, Kashyap and Scharfstein [1990, 1991] and Sheard [1989]), but theoretical literature relating this role to the firm's financial decision is sparse.[62]

This Chapter deals with the firm's choice of capital structure in a financial environment in which the bank's role goes beyond that of a classical intermediary. Our model postulates that the bank is contributing to the task of disciplining a self-interested management. It is widely held that banks in bank-orientated economies play such a role, but in most cases it remains unsettled how this process actually works and what its concrete causalities are. In contrast to many verbal and empirical contributions to this issue, we explicitly state how the presence of the bank affects the prevailing informational friction and what the bank's incentive to exhibit such an activity is.

We present a nested moral hazard problem, in which neither the management's productive action nor the bank's activity in restricting managerial misbehavior is contractible. Instead, both must be provided with incentives to act in the investor's interest. While the incentive scheme for management is a traditional incentive wage schedule, the investor can elicit the bank's activity by taking on debt. This activity is understood as one which decreases management's opportunity cost to exert high effort. One could imagine that the bank's presence with its expertise and specific knowledge about the industry in question is likely to discourage management from acting in a way detrimental to investor's wealth. Thus the bank's participation in the financing of a project has a positive impact on the moral hazard problem between shareholders and management in the sense that lower expected wage payments are necessary to

[61] Examples are Aoki [1994], Baums [1994] or James and Wier [1988]. For an overview with further references see also Garvey and Swan [1994].

[62] An exception is the contribution by Diamond [1991] who is presenting a model in which firms' demand for bank loans originates from this institution's ability to monitor and to alleviate an existing moral hazard problem.

induce a certain effort level of the management. Based on these considerations, our model provides a theory of optimal capital structure in which debt serves as a tool to stimulate the bank to perform a task that an investor is unable to accomplish herself. Section 3.3 will comment on the bank's role in the model and some of the related literature.

One central result of our analysis will be that an investor can substitute sharp monetary incentives by involving a bank which has the ability to make slack less attractive to management. In this respect, we are close to Demougin and Fluet [1997] who consider a principal's choice between monitoring and monetary incentives to elicit an unobservable and onerous action from her agent. Their interpretation of monitoring is, however, much more traditional than the interpretation of bank interference in our model.

The structure of this Chapter will be as follows. Section 2 will lay out our model, while Section 3 will comment in greater depth on the driving assumption of the model, namely that involving a bank into the financing process can alleviate an existing moral hazard problem between investors and management. Section 4 will explain the decision problems of all parties involved (investor, management and bank) which, as we will see, are heavily interconnected. Section 5 develops a procedure to analyze the investor's decision problem and characterizes her optimal choice. The theoretical predictions of our contribution and their compatibility with empirical evidence are presented in Section 6. Section 7 concludes the Chapter with some remarks on empirical observations from the study of Edwards and Fischer [1994] on the German system, which could be brought forward against our model. All proofs can be found in the Appendix to this Chapter.

3.2 The Model

A risk-neutral investor (or a syndicate of investors) is considering whether to start up a project, which requires a fixed investment expenditure of $K > 0$. Control over the project has to be delegated to a risk-averse and effort-averse management, whose unobservable choice of effort influences the distribution over the project's returns. Although the investor has enough funds to pay for the project's set-up cost, she can turn to a bank and ask for credit. the risk-neutral bank has opportunity cost of $(1 + z)$ per Dollar of credit granted to the firm. At the same time this is the rate at which the investor can deposit her money with the bank. The interest rate $(1 + r)$ at which credit is granted will adjust due to banking competition such that the bank's ex-ante expected payoff from participation is 0. How this works deserves further comment, which will be given as soon as the model has been laid out in greater detail.

The manager can choose among two actions a, which we will term for simplicity, "working hard" and "being lazy". Formally, the set of possible actions a is $A = \{p,q\}$ with $p,q \in (0,1)$ and $p > q$. The manager's action determines the probability with which an outcome t from the set of possible outcomes $T = \{0,1\}$ is realized, where p and q constitute probabilities in the following sense $\Pr(t = 1, a = p)$, $\Pr(t = 0, a = p) = (1 - p)$ and $\Pr(t\ 0\ 1, a = q) = q$, $\Pr(t = 0, a = q) = (1 - q)$. $t = 1$ is a favorable event for the investor, since it is affecting the density function from which the random final profit is drawn in a positive way. Let $f(x,t)$ be the continuous density function underlying the firm's random cash flow x at the end of the day with

$$f(x,t) = t \cdot f^H(x) + (1-t) \cdot f^L(x).$$

$f^H(x)$ and $f^L(x)$ are both densities with support $[\underline{x}, \bar{x}]$, where the former function is dominating the latter one in the sense of first-order stochastic dominance, i.e.

$$\int_{\underline{x}}^{\hat{x}} f^H(x)dx \leq \int_{x}^{\hat{x}} f^L(x)dx \qquad \forall \hat{x} \in [\underline{x}, \bar{x}].$$

Concerning the realization of t, one could think about the manager's success in lowering cost, to create a strategic alliance or to implement some business strategy. t is verifiable at the end of the employment relationship between manager and firm.

The investor is unable to observe her manager's choice of action, the result of which is that an employment contract cannot specify a wage as a function of this choice. Action p is beneficial to the investor because it shifts the odds in favor of density function $f^H(x)$, but it is unpleasant to the manager in that this action is more onerous than q. When designing a compensation scheme the investor can restrict herself to the realizations of the discrete random variable t and does not need to refer to the continuous random variable x for that purpose.[63] This knowledge is of great help since one can avoid the difficulties which are associated with continuous wage schedules as described by Hart and Moore [1987] or Jewitt [1988]. Of course it is also possible to base the wage incentives on realizations of x but the investor cannot gain anything by applying a more complicated mechanism. A compensation scheme here will therefore specify a wage for each of the two verifiable realizations in T. Denote these payments by $w(t = 1) = w_1$ and $w(t = 0) = w_0$, respectively.

The risk averse management has a utility function over wage payments given through $u(w)$, which exhibits the properties $u' > 0$ and $u'' < 0$. For technical purposes, we define the utility associated with a payment w_i, $u(w_i)$, as u_i, $i = 0,1$. Furthermore, let the function $h(\cdot)$ be the inverse function of the manager's utility function. This function is monotonically increasing in wage payments as well and strictly convex by the underlying assumptions on the manager's utility function. Management must at least derive an expected minimum utility level of $\underline{u}$ from its employment, or it will refuse to take the job.

The manager incurs a disutility from choosing action p, $d(p)$ and one from choosing action q which is given by $d(q,b)$. The latter disutility is influenced by the bank's activity level b. The bank's activity shall be understood as one which makes slack less attractive to the management, for instance intensively seeking information about the firm and its policy. The bank could acquire this information through its representation on the supervisory board or, if such an institution does not exist, through other channels. Intensity of this action could

[63] This is the case, since t is a sufficient statistic in the sense of Holmström [1979, 84].

depend (among other things) on the amount of bank internal staff delegated to deal with issues concerning the firm.

If the bank is involved in the project with a decent sum of money, it will require some sort of intermediate reports and briefings on the project's progress. A hard working management may have generated the documentation of the project as a side product, while a lazy management will have to engage in some extra work to cover up its laziness, be it by "cooking the books" or by falsifying some evidence of its indolence. the more intense the bank's activity becomes (i.e. the more information it has gathered), the higher the manager's disutility from being lazy (i.e. management is at greater pains to hide its slackness). To put it in different terms, the opportunity cost of working hard will decrease in *b*.

Assume that the bank can choose its level of activity, *b*, from the finite set $B = \{0, b_1, ..., b_N\}$, with $0 < b_I < ... < b_N < \infty$. The bank's activity increases the management's disutility of choosing the less onerous action *q*, but there isn't any level of *b* – no matter how large – which can make the manager's disutility from choosing *q* larger than that from choosing *p*, i.e. assume

$$d(p) > d(q, b = b_N) > d(q, b = b_{N-1}) > ... > d(q, b = 0),$$

with $d(q, b = 0) \geq 0$.

Exerting an activity level *b* is costly for the bank, where accruing cost can be described by a function $C = C(b)$ with discrete domain B. The function $C(b)$ is strictly increasing in *b*, with $C(0) = 0$. Furthermore assume that

$$(p-q) \cdot \left[\int_{\underline{x}}^{\bar{x}} x \cdot \left(f^H(x) - f^L(x) \right) dx \right] - C(b_N) \geq 0.$$

Speaking in economic terms, this means that the expected increase in gross payoff of switching from *q* to *p* is larger than the cost of the bank's highest activity level.

Just as the investor cannot choose the management's effort directly, she also cannot directly choose the bank's activity level. A possible justification for this assumption is that the bank's measures to bring about a certain intensity b may be in fact be very complicated and the investor lacks the needed expertise to determine what the appropriate measures are. The delegation of this action to the financial institution is therefore assumed to be inevitable.

In contrast to an ordinary principal-agent framework, we encounter two moral hazard problems here. The investor (the principal) has two agents (management and the bank). The first agent (management) is in charge of the firm's operating decision, while the action of the latter agent (the bank) influences the severeness of the informational friction prevailing in the relationship between the first agent and the principal. This interrelation of the two problems is similar to a model by Varian [1990] in which agents are employed to monitor other agents. He considers the interesting case of group monitoring schemes in the course of a bank's lending to small farmers in developing countries such as Bangladesh. These loans are made to groups of farmers who influence each other's cost of engaging in actions which are either detrimental or to the benefit of the joint project's expected return.

In our model, no activity of any agent can be contracted upon and therefore both agents must be provided with the appropriate incentives to act in the investor's interest. Inducing hard work on behalf of the management seems to be a straightforward task, since the investor can set the incentives for the management by the compensation scheme. Setting the incentives for the bank however is less obvious. The way to elicit a desired activity level from the bank is to create in it an interest in the firm's business. Here, this will be achieved by taking on debt. In order to solve the investor's decision problem, we must analyze how the choice of the wage schedule and debt influences the decision problems of the two agents at the subsequent stages. This will be done in the following Section, before we turn to the investor's problem. To understand how the decision problems fit together, we will first present a rough sketch of the model's timing.

The model is set up in four stages. At the initial stage, the investor simultaneously chooses a wage incentive schedule for the management and makes a decision on the financing of the firm. The financial decision involves a debt level D and an interest rate $(1 + r)$ at which the investor wishes to take on this debt. This loan contract (a certain debt level D granted at an interest rate $(1+r)$) and management's monetary incentives are exogenously given at the second stage, when it comes to the bank to make its decisions. The world ends, if the bank refuses to grant the credit D at the proposed interest rate $(1 + r)$. Otherwise the bank makes a decision about b. After the bank has made its decision, the manager has to decide whether or not to participate in the third stage. If he is willing to work under the prevailing conditions, notably the specified wage contract and the bank activity b, he must make a decision whether to work hard or not. Again the world ends if the manager is not willing to sign the wage contract. At the fourth and final stage, the realization of t determines from which distribution the firm's profit x is drawn. The continuous random variable x takes on its value immediately after the realization of t. Both realizations are verifiable. It depends on the latter realization, whether the firm is able to meet its debt obligation or not. If x is insufficient to service the outstanding debt obligation, the bank takes over control and cashes in all receipts. In the event the firm is able to repay its debt, management repays the loan and the investor receives the remaining funds.

3.3 On the Bank's Role in the Model

The role of the bank in the above model is not productive in the sense that its action improves on the management's choice in any way (the bank's action does not shift the odds in favor of the investor). Therefore, the bank is by no means playing a consultancy function as put forward by Edwards and Fischer [1994, 197] for the German economy. The bank's activity bears its effect purely on the informational friction between the investor and management. More specifically, it influences management's opportunity cost of exerting the onerous action which the investor wants it to take. The question is whether this modelling is indeed a truthful reflection of the empirical evidence and existing institutional arrangements in bank-oriented economies. To clarify these issues, there are two points that deserve some comments. First of all, what concrete actions of the bank lead to this effect on managerial cost to engage in one or the other action? Secondly, one has to answer the connected question of how the alteration of the agent's cost structure is brought about.

Aoki [1994, 134] distinguishes three types of bank monitoring vis-à-vis firms to which credit has been granted: ex-ante, interim and ex-post monitoring. Ex-ante monitoring refers to a bank's activity towards assessing a firm's credit-worthiness in a broad sense. This monitoring includes gathering information about the project to be undertaken, its probability of success, the qualification of the management, the position of the firm in the market and the like. Interim monitoring refers to checking the project and the management while the project is being undertaken. For example, after the bank has granted a credit to finance some machinery, it may interfere and ask for changes if the money is not being used in the way agreed upon initially. Finally, ex-post monitoring refers to the verification of project returns especially in the case of project failure. When we speak of monitoring in the present model we have in mind ex-ante an interim monitoring.

One characteristic of the Japanese economy is that many firms belong to an industrial group (the so-called *keiretsu*), which is centered around a main bank. As Sheard [1989, 403] notes, a firm within such a relationship "will provide regular reports on its performance" to the bank. He goes on to state that "the bank is able to obtain inside access to the firm and its internal decision-making, allowing it to obtain information about the firm and its management which is not readily available, or available only at high cost, to the external capital market" (Sheard [1989, 403]). For the German system, Cable [1985, 119] states that there is a "substantial flow of information about corporate plans and performance" to banks, and Edwards and Fischer [1994, 147] point to a similar information flow in the course of the assessment process prior to a loan and during the implementation phase of the project. This information transmission might be supported by the frequent representation of German banks on client firms' supervisory boards.

It is the intensity of this information gathering, manifesting itself for example in the number of bank internal staff delegated to this task or the number of hours dedicated to this endeavor, which we have in mind with the bank's activity level b. b may be interpreted as ex-ante as well as interim monitoring in the sense of Aoki [1994, 134], though the latter type of monitoring is more consistent with the set-up of the model. Now the question is how this activity can increase management's cost of being lazy. In anticipation of bank intervention on shareholder meetings (perceived to be unpleasant by management), management may feel the need to conceal the fact that it did not take great pains in order to positively influence the firm's prospects.[64] For this reason, slackness may be less attractive than in the case in which there is nobody with enough expertise to judge whether the current firm policy is well chosen or not. This view follows Baums [1994, 417], who argues that management's "knowledge of being observed may influence behavior".

Our view on the monitoring role of banks has to be contrasted with the fact that delegated monitoring does not necessarily have to be tied to lending or financial intermediation in general. Rating agencies for example evaluate and monitor firms, without being involved into their business in any way. Dewatripont and Tirole [1993] argue that rating agencies engage in monitoring and produce reliable information in order to keep a good reputation as a reliable source of information. The driving force behind monitoring is completely different in our setting here. The bank engages in monitoring in our model since it has a fixed stake in the firm (in terms of the credit granted). This view on the bank's incentive to monitor will be explained further below.

3.4 The Sequence of Decision Problems

3.4.1 The Management

Management chooses its payoff maximizing action at the third stage of the model. This choice will depend on the prevailing monetary incentives chosen by

[64] Aoki [1990, 15] is describing this intervention into a firm's business as soon as performance gets poor for the Japanese economy.

the investor in the initial stage and on the bank behavior during the second stage. For simplicity we assume that wage payments are not made out of current receipts, but out of the investor's private pocket. this assumption is not fundamental to the analysis, but makes the exposition much easier. Note that therefore the loan contract does not directly enter the management's decision problem.

Given that the management does accept the investor's job offer, its utility maximization problem at this point in time is simply to choose the most attractive action from the set of available actions $A = \{p,q\}$. In the following we will assume that the investor's most preferred action is p. If this wasn't the case, the problem would not be interesting, since there are no incentives necessary to implement q. Now, if action p is to be implemented, a minimum requirement on the wage schedule chosen is the following condition:

$$p \cdot u_1 + (1-p) \cdot u_0 - d(p) - \underline{u} \geq 0.$$

We will refer to this condition as the manager's participation constraint. Given that the investor wants to implement p, it must be the case that the manager is choosing this action voluntarily, i.e. this choice must be incentive compatible for him. This is captured by the condition

$$p \cdot u_1 + (1-p) \cdot u_0 - d(p) \geq q \cdot u_1 + (1-q) \cdot u_0 - d(q,b),$$

which is the so-called incentive constraint.

3.4.2 The Bank

The bank's behavior in the second stage of the model is dependent on three then exogenously given parameters. First, the bank is aware of the monetary incentives (u_0, u_1) that were specified for the management. Second and third, the proposed loan contract from the first period involving D and an interest rate $(1 + r)$. The bank has now two options. Either it chooses not to grant the loan in which case it will receive a payoff of 0, or it agrees to grant credit at the specified terms. In this latter case it will then proceed to choose its payoff-maximizing activity level b.

But what is the bank's incentive to pursue some function on the supervisory board or to engage in some costly information gathering? Given that the bank grants the loan, it has a fixed stake in the firm and is interested in recovering the funds lent plus the agreed repayment. activity b can influence the manager's choice in favor of hard work, as one can see from the manager's incentive constraint and the bank can benefit from such an activity if this tips the odds in favor of repayment.

The decision of the bank at this point in time depends on whether it is rather interested in implementation of p or q. It might not be within the bank's power to influence the manager's choice of action, but if it is, the set of bank activity levels supporting an implementation of some $a \in A$ crucially depend on the wage schedule (u_0, u_1) which is then exogenously given.[65] Given that the bank is in a position to induce either one of the actions, the cheapest way to induce q is to choose $b = 0$, since the manager's incentive constraint is then not of any relevance. Parallel to that, the cheapest way to induce p is to choose the minimum b, which elicits this choice from the manager, given some specified (u_0, u_1).

Definition 2 Provided a wage schedule (u_0, u_1) and some $b \in \mathrm{B}$ are able to implement the managerial action p, then denote the minimum level of bank activity, necessary to implement p at this specific wage contract (u_0, u_1) by

$$b^{Min}(u_0, u_1) = \min\{\, b \in \mathrm{B} \,|\, (p-q)\cdot u_1 - (p-q)\cdot u_0 - d(p) + d(q,b) \geq 0 \,\}.$$

The notation is parallel to the one adopted in Chapter 2, where the manager was risk neutral. Expected bank payoff at some given loan contract $(D, (1 + r))$ in the case with $a = p$ and $b = b^{Min}(u_0, u_1)$ is

[65] The bank is not able to bring about an implementation of p if the manager's incentive constraint is not satisfied at the given wage schedule given b_N. On the other hand, if the prevailing wage schedule is already implementing p at the lowest bank activity $b = 0$, the bank cannot affect the manager's incentives, no matter what its activity level is.

$$\pi^B\left(b=b^{Min}(u_0,u_1)\right)=p\cdot\int_{\underline{x}}^{D\cdot(1+r)} x\cdot f^H(x)dx+D\cdot(1+r)\cdot\int_{D\cdot(1+r)}^{\bar{x}} f^H(x)dx$$

$$+(1-p)\cdot\left[\int_{\underline{x}}^{D\cdot(1+r)} x\cdot f^L(x)dx+D\cdot(1+r)\cdot\int_{D\cdot(1+r)}^{\bar{x}} f^L(x)dx\right] \tag{3.1}$$

$$-C\left(b^{Min}(u_0,u_1)\right)-D\cdot(1+z),$$

while in the case with $a=q$ and $b=0$ it is given through

$$\pi^B(b=0)=q\cdot\left[\int_{\underline{x}}^{D\cdot(1+r)} x\cdot f^H(x)dx+D\cdot(1+r)\cdot\int_{D\cdot(1+r)}^{\bar{x}} f^H(x)dx\right]$$

$$+(1-q)\cdot\left[\int_{\underline{x}}^{D\cdot(1+r)} x\cdot f^L(x)dx+D\cdot(1+r)\cdot\int_{D\cdot(1+r)}^{\bar{x}} f^L(x)dx\right] \tag{3.2}$$

$$-C(b=0)-D\cdot(1+z).$$

As an explanation for the two expressions, note that the bank cashes in all receipts from the project in case of bankruptcy and obtains the agreed repayment if funds are sufficient to service the debt obligations. These two events may occur for each possible density function. $D\cdot(1+z)$ captures the bank's opportunity cost of the loan.

Whether the bank truly wants to bring about an implementation of p is a different matter. For this to be the case it must be true that the bank's expected payoff as given through expression (3.1) must be larger than the one given in expression (3.2), or in formal terms

$$(p-q)\cdot\left[\int_{\underline{x}}^{D\cdot(1+r)} x\cdot\left(f^H(x)-f^L(x)\right)dx\right.$$

$$\left.+D\cdot(1+r)\cdot\int_{D\cdot(1+r)}^{\bar{x}}\left(f^H(x)-f^L(x)\right)dx\right] \qquad \text{(Bank-IC)}$$

$$\geq C\left(b^{Min}(u_0,u_1)\right).$$

The bank will only accept a proposed combination of wage schedule (u_0, u_1) and loan contract involving some credit D and interest rate $(1 + r)$, if the expected payoff at its payoff maximizing choice b^* under these parameters exceeds its refinancing cost of $D\cdot(1 + z)$, i.e. if

$$\pi^B\left(D,(1+r),b^*(D,(1+r),(u_0,u_1))\right)\geq D\cdot(1+z).^{66} \qquad \text{(Bank-PC)}$$

This constitutes the bank's participation constraint. Bank competition in the first stage of the model will allow the investor to obtain a loan D at an interest rate $(1 + r)$ which leaves the bank with a zero profit at its profit maximizing choice of b. The determination of the interest rate will be discussed in more detail below. As can already be seen from the bank's incentive constraint, managerial incentives will play a crucial role in the determination of the terms at which credit is granted.

3.4.3 The Investor

The investor's decision variables in the first stage of the model are the loan contract $(D,(1+r))$ and wage schedule (u_0,u_1). Since she can neither command her agent to take action p, nor directly influence the bank's activity level, she must choose the parameters at her disposal to induce bank and management to exhibit the desired behavior. Her aim is to minimize the implementation cost of

---

[66] Of course an optimal choice b^* is existing for any combination of D, $(1 + r)$ and (u_0,u_1) by virtue of the finiteness of B.

her most desired managerial effort level p through a diligent choice of (u_0, u_1) and the financial decision. This analysis appears extremely complicated, since the decision problems are so heavily intertwined. Notably, the determination of the interest rate at which the loan is initially taken on seems to pose a real problem. The choice of the manager's wage contract will determine what activity level the bank must exert to induce p. That is, the bank's optimal choice of b depends on (u_0, u_1). But since the interest rate at the payoff maximizing choice (given D) must be such that the bank is left with a zero profit, this rate will also depend on the managerial incentive schedule. This seems to make an analysis of the investor's problem almost impossible.

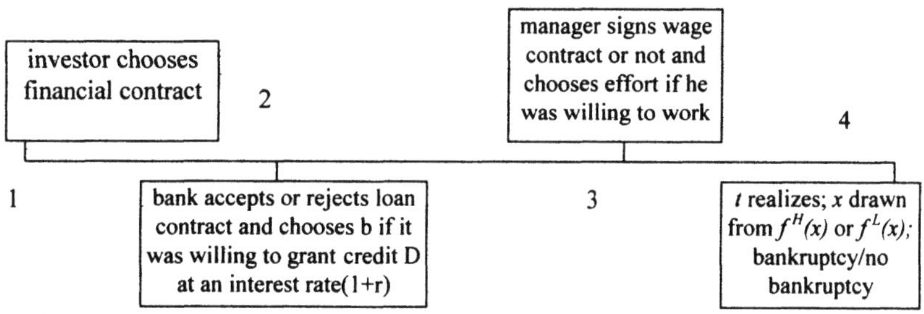

Figure 3.1: Timing of Events.

These kind of problems can be avoided if we divide the problem into three parts. In a first part, the investor must find an optimal wage contract for each combination of managerial effort and bank activity level, (p,b) with $b \in \mathrm{B}$. The second step is to determine the loan contract for each combination (p,b) such that the bank voluntarily exhibits an activity level of b and makes a zero profit at this choice. In a third step, the investor must choose a combination (p,b^*) among all tupels $(p,b), b \in \mathrm{B}$, which maximizes her expected payoff from running the firm. The optimal financing of the firm D^* is then the one which is associated with her most preferred choice (p,b^*). Before we turn to this analysis in greater detail, let us repeat the timing of the model for reasons of clarity.

3.5 Analysis of the Model

This Section will present the three steps of the investor's maximization problem. The first step will show that there exists a unique cost-minimizing wage schedule to implement a managerial action of p given any $b \in \mathrm{B}$. The second step will then demonstrate that incentives for the bank can be set in such a way that this institution is willing to exhibit the activity level of b voluntarily given that some wage contract $(u_0^*(b), u_1^*(b))$ $b \in \mathrm{B}$ was chosen. In the third step, the investor must choose the vector $\left(\left(u_0^*(b^*), \left(u_1^*(b^*)\right), b^*, D^*\right)$ that implements her most desired managerial action p most cost effectively. This structure resembles the two-step procedure presented, for example, in Kreps [1990, 587].

3.5.1 Step 1: Minimization of Expected Wage Payments

Although we have assumed that the investor cannot directly influence the bank's activity level, we will start from the benchmark case in which she can choose monetary incentives and b. In this situation, the cost of implementing managerial action p consists of expected wage payments and the cost accrued through exercising activity b. The sum of both is referred to as implementation cost C_p. This first step seeks to derive implementation cost of p under any b from B.

Her expected payoff (given there exists an incentive scheme which achieves an implementation of p), is characterized by the following expression

$$\pi^I = p \cdot \left[\int_{\underline{x}}^{\overline{x}} x \cdot f^H(x) dx \right] + (1-p) \cdot \left[\int_{\underline{x}}^{\overline{x}} x \cdot f^L(x) dx \right] - C_p .$$

As one can see, payoff maximization is equivalent to a minimization of expected implementation cost C_p.

The minimization problem, which the investor must solve in this first step, is the following. For each $b \in \mathrm{B}$

$$\max_{u_0,u_1} \; -p\cdot h(u_1)-(1-p)\cdot h(u_0)-C(b)$$

s.t.

$$p\cdot u_1+(1-p)\cdot u_0-d(p)-\underline{u}\geq 0 \qquad \text{(PC)}$$

and

$$(p-q)\cdot u_1-(p-q)\cdot u_0-d(p)+d(q,b)\geq 0, \qquad \text{(IC)}$$

where u_0 and u_1 are both chosen from the set of real numbers **R**. In words, the investor's problem is to minimize the cost of implementing action p subject to the management's participation and incentive constraint, which have already been explained above. The Lagrangian and the Kuhn-Tucker conditions for this problem can be found in the Appendix.

Proposition 4 For each $b\in \mathrm{B}$ there exists a vector $\left(u_0^*,u_1^*\right)$, which achieves implementation of the investor's most preferred action p at minimum cost C_p^{Min}.

Proof: See Appendix. ■

This wage schedule has the property that $u_0<u_1$ which is also shown in the Appendix. Apart from that and the mere existence of such a vector, we can specify explicitly, how the incentive schedule must look.

Proposition 5 At some given $b\in \mathrm{B}$ the wage schedule $\left(u_0^*,u_1^*\right)$ is unique and characterized by $u_0^*(b)=\dfrac{p\cdot d(q,b)-q\cdot d(p)}{(p-q)}+\underline{u}$, and

$u_1^*\left(b=\dfrac{(1-q)\cdot d(p)-(1-p)\cdot d(q,b)}{(p-q)}\right)+\underline{u}$. **Proof:** See Appendix. ■

Definition 3 Denote by $(u_0^*(b)\,u_1^*(b))$ the optimal contract that achieves implementation of p at minimum wage cost $p\cdot h(u_1^*(b))+(1-p)\cdot h(u_2^*(b))$ given b. U_B denotes the set of all optimal contracts for $b\in \mathrm{B}$.

What can one learn from the analysis of this benchmark case that allows the investor to choose the wage schedule *and* the parameter *b*? Most importantly, we do see that there exists a globally optimal way to implement action *p*, if both devices are under the investor's discretion. Unfortunately, the investor cannot choose *b* directly, but the bank must be provided with appropriate incentives to choose the level *b*, on which the maximization problem to find $(u_0^*(b), u_1^*(b))$ was based upon. If it was possible to show that for each $u(b) \in U_B$ the bank can be provided with incentives to exhibit the level *b*, we are done. This is because the globally optimal way to implement *p* is among the alternative ways of implementation found in step 1.

3.5.2 Step 2: Implementation of *b* given $(u_0^*(b), u_1^*(b))$

First of all, note that at any contract $u(\hat{b}) \in U_B$ the manager's incentive constraint is binding. Thus, the bank's activity level is essential for an implementation of *p* in the sense that any activity level strictly below will fail to support an implementation of *p*. In terms of our notation introduced above we can state that

$$b = b^{Min}\left(u_0^*(b), u_1^*(b)\right) \qquad \forall b \in \mathrm{B}. \tag{3.3}$$

Abstracting from any incentive issues to elicit a certain bank activity *b*, there is a certain upper bound on debt *D* which can be taken on at some $b \in \mathrm{B}$. This maximum amount can be derived from the following considerations.

Debt is riskless as long as it is below $\underline{x}/(1+z)$, and it becomes risky as soon as it surpasses this critical threshold. Note that the bank will not accept any credit which requires a repayment in excess of the project's maximum possible return $\bar{x}$. Provided action *p* is implemented, this defines a maximum debt level

$$D^{Max}(b =)\frac{p \cdot \int_{\underline{x}}^{\bar{x}} x \cdot f^H(x)dx + (1-p) \cdot \int_{\underline{x}}^{\bar{x}} x \cdot f^L(x)dx - C(b)}{(1+z)},$$

which the investor can take on at the bank's activity level of b. Our assumption concerning the increase in expected return associated with a switch p to q implies that the set of admissible debt levels at any b that the investor might head for, is non-empty.

We have already mentioned that the bank will not be willing to participate if it cannot hope for a payoff which is at least as great as the opportunity cost of the demanded loan. Apart from that, we have repeatedly referred to banking competition as the determining factor of the interest rate (1 + r). These issues shall be taken up now.

Fix some $u(b) \in U_B$ and a debt level $D \in [0, D^{Max}(b)]$ and assume for a moment that the bank is voluntarily choosing the desired b. The investor can now propose an interest rate at which the bank does not receive any expected payoff in excess of its opportunity cost $D \cdot (1+z)$, i.e. at $b = b^{Min}\left(u_0^*(b,)u_1^*(b)\right)$, the interest rate (1 + r) will adjust such that

$$p \cdot \left[\int_{\underline{x}}^{D\cdot(1+r)} x \cdot f^H(x)dx + D \cdot (1+r) \cdot \int_{D\cdot(1+r)}^{\bar{x}} f^H(x)dx \right]$$

$$+ (1-p) \cdot \left[\int_{\underline{x}}^{D\cdot(1+r)} x \cdot f^L(x)dx + D \cdot (1+r) \cdot \int_{D\cdot(1+r)}^{\bar{x}} f^L(x)dx \right]$$

$$- C(b) - D \cdot (1+z) = 0$$

(1 + r) is then a function of D, but from the last expression it also becomes clear that the interest rate will depend on b. In the end, the bank has to choose b voluntarily, and therefore $(1+r)$ will also depend on the prevailing managerial incentives. It seems that we are encountering the same problems which we attempted to circumvent initially. The very reason why we broke up the investor's maximization problem, was to avoid the dependence of the interest rate on managerial incentives, which is what we find here.

Note however that matters are now much simpler. We are confronted with a finite rather than an infinite number of managerial wage schedules. For some given b and an associated $\left(u_0^*(b,)u_1^*(b)\right)$ we can therefore quite easily analyze the interest rate behavior for varying D.

It is shown in the Appendix that the interest rate (given that the bank chooses a fixed b from B) that leaves the bank with a zero profit is an increasing function in D. This does not take into account that there is an incentive problem and that the bank cannot be forced to choose a certain activity level. However, this result is an intermediate step towards an optimal choice of D with respect to the design of the appropriate incentives for the bank.

The procedure to establish incentive compatibility for this institution is as follows: For each wage contract $\left(u_0^*(b), u_1^*(b)\right) \in U_B$ the investor must choose debt level D in such a way that the bank's incentive constraint for a choice of this specific b is satisfied, of course taking into account how the interest rate changes as D changes. Since we do know the behavior of $(1+r)$ in D given b, it is only one last step to establish incentive compatibility for the bank.

In order to ensure that the bank is indeed choosing $b = b^{Min}(u(b))$ at given $u(b) \in U_B$, it must be the case that

$$(p-q)\cdot\left[\int_{\underline{x}}^{D\cdot(1+r(b,D))} x\cdot\left(f^H(x)-f^L(x)\right)dx\right.$$

$$\left.+D\cdot(1+r)\cdot(b,D)\cdot\int_{D\cdot(1+r(b,D))}^{\bar{x}}\left(f^H(x)-f^L(x)\right)dx\right]-C(b)\geq 0$$

Here is where the partition of the maximization problem does the trick. We can exogenously fix b at some level in B (and thus by implication some $(u_0^*(b), u_1^*(b))$ and afterwards ask the question what debt level is needed to make the choice of b incentive compatible for the bank. It is possible to state the following:

Proposition 6 For each $u(\hat{b}) \in U_B$ there is existing a debt level $\hat{D}$, such that the bank's unique payoff maximizing choice of b from the set B is $\hat{b}$ bank's expected payoff at this choice is 0.

Proof: See Appendix. ■

The first term on the left-hand side of the bank's incentive constraint is 0 at $D =$ 0 and increasing in D (by the results about the behavior of the interest rate D given some specified b). All the investor must do is to choose D sufficiently large to make the choice of $\hat{b}$ incentive compatible for the bank. There is an upper bound on maximum debt level that is acceptable to the bank given a certain b but, as shown in the Appendix, this does not cause an existence problem of $\hat{D}$ for implementation of $\hat{b}$.

Unfortunately, the debt level, which brings about incentive compatibility for the bank is not unique. Rather, there is an entire interval of debt levels, which induce the bank to choose the desired activity level. For any tupel $(u^*(b), b)$ this interval ranges from a minimum debt level $D^{Min}(b)$ implicitly defined by the bank's binding inventive constraint to the maximum admissible debt level under an activity level b, given by $D^{Max}(b)$. We adopt the following definition.

Definition 4 For each $b \in B$ and the associated wage schedule $(u_0^*(b), u_1^*(b))$ the minimum amount of debt $D^{Min}(b)$ which is able to establish incentive compatibility for the choice of b is implicitly given through

$$(p-q)\cdot\left[\int_{\underline{x}}^{D\cdot(1+r(b,D))} x\cdot\left(f^H(x)-f^L(x)\right)dx\right.$$

$$\left.+D\cdot(1+r(b,D))\cdot\int_{D\cdot(1+r(b,D))}^{\bar{x}}\left(f^H(x)-f^L(x)\right)dx\right]$$

$$=C(b),$$

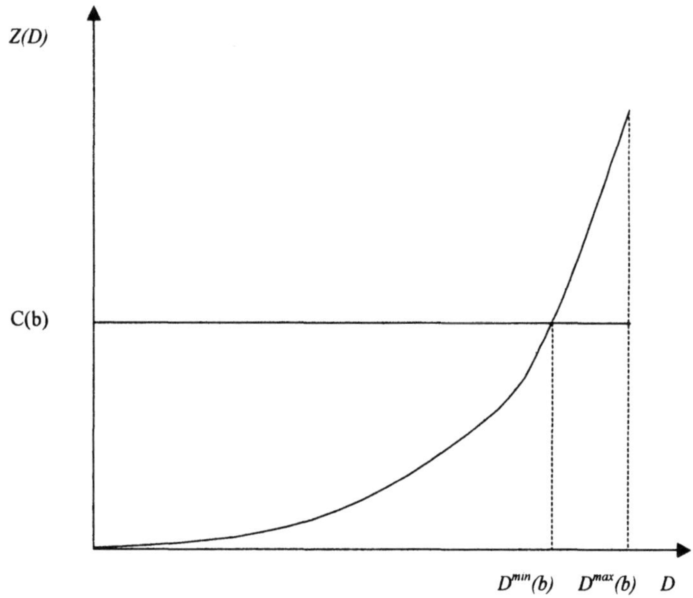

Figure 3.2: The Optimal Choice of Debt.

where the function r(b,D) is determined as described in the Appendix. Denote the LHS of this last equation by Z(D).

Figure 3.2 gives a graphical illustration of the last Proposition graphing *D* on the abscissa and *Z(D)* on the ordinate.

3.5.3 Step 3: Investor's Payoff Maximization

As we have seen above, there exists a globally optimal way to implement *p* if wage schedule and activity *b* are both under the investor's discretion. Step 2 of our partitioned maximization problem has shown that the investor can indeed induce the bank to exert any *b* given a wage schedule associated with that bank activity level. But this means that the investor can now simply choose the cheapest way of implementation among all alternatives derived in step 1.

Imagine that the investor has decided to implement p through a certain bank activity of b. This immediately implies an optimal wage schedule $\left(u_0^*(b,)u_1^*(b)\right)$. Furthermore the investor must take on debt D from the interval $[D^{Min}(b), D^{Max}(b)]$ and her expected payoff at some interest rate $(1+r)$ will then be

$$\pi^1 =$$

$$p \cdot \left[\int_{D\cdot(1+r)}^{\bar{x}} x \cdot f^H(x)dx - D\cdot(1+r) \cdot \int_{D\cdot(1+r)}^{\bar{x}} f^H(x)dx \right]$$

$$+ (1-p) \cdot \left[\int_{D\cdot(1+r)}^{\bar{x}} x \cdot f^L(x)dx - D\cdot(1+r) \cdot \int_{D\cdot(1+r)}^{\bar{x}} f^L(x)dx \right] - (K-D)\cdot(1+z).$$

The firm may either be in a position to repay the loan or not. If it is not in financial distress the investor will receive what is left over after debt obligation has been serviced. Apart from that, the investor has opportunity cost of $(1+z)$ per Dollar invested into the project. This is what the last line states. Remember that the investor can propose a loan contract involving an interest rate $(1+r)$ which leaves the bank with a zero profit, i.e. with a binding participation constraint.

Making use of this information, we solve the bank's binding incentive constraint for the term $D\cdot(1+z)$ by plugging it into the above expression. One then arrives at

$$\pi^I = p \cdot \left[\int_{\underline{x}}^{\bar{x}} x \cdot f^H(x)dx \right] + (1-p) \cdot \left[\int_{\underline{x}}^{\bar{x}} f^L(x)dx \right] - C_p,$$

which is the starting point of step 1.

Thus, the investor's basic choice is to decide, which activity level of the bank $b \in \mathrm{B}$ is minimizing the implementation cost C_p according to

$$\underset{b \in \mathrm{B}}{Max} - p \cdot h\left(u_1^*(b)\right) - (1-p) \cdot h\left(u_0^*(b)\right) - C(b),$$

with $(u_0^*(b), u_1^*(b)) \in U_B$. The fact that there exists an optimal wage schedule implementing p at any b of course implies that there exists a solution to the investor's overall problem by virtue of the finiteness of B. Debt level D must be chosen to make activity level b incentive compatible for the bank. The investor's optimal choice can thus finally be stated as follows.

Proposition 7 The investor's optimal choice is characterized by a vector

$$\left(u_0^*(b^*,)u_1^*(b^*)\right),\ b^*, D^*,$$

with $b^* \in \underset{b \in \mathrm{B}}{\arg\min}\, p \cdot h\left(u_1^*(b)\right) + (1-p) \cdot h\left(u_0^*(b)\right) + C(b), \left(u_0^*(b), u_1^*(b)\right) \in U_b$ and

the optimal debt level $D^* \in [D^{Min}(b), D^{Max}(b)]$

Proof: By step 1 and 2. ■

As in the case of the two-step procedure, there is no hope of obtaining uniqueness concerning the action level at the bank in this third step of our partitioned maximization problem. there is also a multiplicity of debt levels. One could argue that the focal debt level is the minimum debt level able to bring about incentive compatibility for the bank, but our model does not provide any grounds for such an argument.

3.6 Bank Corporate Control vs. Monetary Incentives

Although our model does not generate any clear-cut theoretical prediction with respect to the investor's decision, it is possible to extract one general result concerning the relationship between the sharpness of wage schedules and the implemented level of bank activity.

Proposition 8 Optimal wage schedules become less high-powered as the bank's activity level increases in the sense that $\Delta u = u_1^*(b) - u_0^*(b)$is strictly decreasing in b.

Proof: Directly follows from Proposition (5). ■

This relates the two governance devices of bank activity and executive compensation to each other, but the firm's financing decision stands behind the bank's involvement in the firm's business. As we see, a high activity level *b* can substitute for high-powered incentives coming from managerial remuneration. this prediction can be tested in regard to its compatibility with empirical evidence. Firms in a bank-oriented financial system should exhibit top executive compensation schemes which are less high-powered than those adopted by comparable companies in a market-based system. empirical evidence is indeed compatible with this predicted pattern. Executive pay in Japan and Germany is not as dependent on success as it is in Anglo-Saxon countries.[67]

Although our theoretical results are compatible with empirical findings, we must be careful to interpret this evidence according to our model. The differences in the sharpness of monetary incentives across various countries need not be necessarily related to the trade-off that our model suggests. Another justification for emphasis of the success-dependent component of pay in some countries could be that social consensus in such countries attaches more importance to the maximization of shareholder wealth than it does in other countries. as an indication for that point, one might take the existence of mechanisms like security class actions in the US (an extremely powerful tool to ensure implementation of shareholders' interest) and contrast it to the relatively

[67] Kaplan [1994, 513] notes that monetary incentives for Japanese top executives are not as high-powered as compared to those of US top managers. this manifests itself in the percentage of managerial stock ownership in the managed firm which is only half as high for Japanese managers as compared to top executives in the US. Consult Herzel [1987a] for executive compensation schedules in the US as compared to Japan and Germany or Greiler [1997] for some anecdotal evidence on the lack of strong monetary incentives within German firms as compared to the US. A further reference on these issues is Milgrom and Roberts [1992, 442-3] who are commenting on managerial compensation from an international perspective.

strong representation of labor unions (for example as compared to banks) on supervisory boards of large German firms.[68]

3.7 Conclusion

This Chapter has presented a model in which the bank's activity can lead to alleviating an existing moral hazard problem between firm management and investor. It is a common argument in corporate governance literature that banks do indeed play such a role in bank-oriented economies but one can hardly find formal models that attempt to pin down the exact causality of this role. Our contribution is an attempt to fill this gap and to provide a basis for further discussion on this topic. There may be several objections to our model. Most basically, one can of course doubt whether the bank's presence in the project does indeed have an effect on the agent's cost structure of choosing different actions. Given one is willing to accept that, there remain other objections on empirical grounds, those for example raised in the studies by Edwards and Fischer [1994] and Edwards and Nibel [1998].

Edwards and Fischer [1994, 130 and 214] doubt whether the average number of shareholder meetings of large AGs in Germany (approximately two times a year – the legal minimum number) indeed allows the bank to be well informed about internal business plans and company decision-making. This can be countered by arguing that the mere number of meetings does not say much about the bank's endeavor to scrutinizing firm policy, especially given that information transmission is not restricted to those meetings. On the contrary. It is unlikely that bank activity only takes on the form of attending such meetings. One would expect that banks remain active in information gathering, for example, about the firm's industry and other profit relevant factors.[69]

---

[68] Consult Shleifer and Vishny [1997] for more information concerning security class actions in the US. According to Emmons and Schmid [1998, 27] 14% of supervisory board seats of the 100 largest German firms were held by labor union executives in 1993. As compared to that only 9% of the seats were held by banks.

[69] This activity might also take on the form of a close link to firm executives. such an ongoing contact between company and bank is extensively described in Sheard [1989] for the case of Japan.

Edwards and Fischer [1994, 136] report that 75% of the 100 largest German AGs have bank representatives on their supervisory board, but they also state that the average number of representatives is actually quite low.[70] In their opinion, representation is not large enough to influence firm's behavior to a significant extent. One can reply to this objection that again the mere number of representatives does not allow such a conclusion, since the bank is likely to hold a more important seat than the average supervisory board representative. this may be the case – as Edwards and Fischer themselves recognize – if the bank can assemble a significant amount of proxy voting or it can wield control over the firm through the outstanding loans.[71]

As an empirical fact, the market for loans in Germany is very competitive (Edwards and Fischer [1994, 142-3]) which does not seem to leave much possibilities for house banks to extract higher interest margins on loans. This may cast doubt on a bank's overall incentive to engage in the role of a corporate monitor. The assumption of a competitive loan market is, however, not in contradiction to house bank relationships and the corporate governance role of the bank. this becomes obvious from our model, which builds upon the assumption of a perfectly competitive banking market as a basic starting point. Incentives do not originate from excessive returns but from the fact that a granted loan has to be safeguarded through appropriate measures while final profit is indeed 0.

We believe that the main contribution of our work lies in providing a theoretical link between the corporate governance role of banks and financing on the one side and executive compensation on the other. Our model suggests that close bank-firm links are able to be substituted for high-powered incentive schemes. This result seems to be confirmed by empirical evidence concerning bank involvement and monetary incentives in the two financial systems. Firms tend to rely more on sharp executive remuneration in Anglo-Saxon countries, while

[70] See again the data on supervisory board composition of German firms given in Emmons and Schmid [1998, 27].

[71] See Edwards and Nibel [1998] on this issue. Their study investigates whether the bank's ability to exercise proxy votes has a positive impact on returns. The authors oppose the view that this is the case for the German economy.

at the same time the corporate governance role of banks is rather negligible. In contrast, executive compensation plans in countries with a bank-oriented system are rather low-powered.

3.8 Appendix

3.8.1 Lagrangian and FOCs

Given some $b \in \mathrm{B}$, the Lagrangian of the investor's problem is:

$$\begin{aligned} L(u_0, u_1; \lambda_{PC}, \lambda_{IC}) \quad = \quad & -p \cdot h(u_1) - (1-p) \cdot h(u_0) - C(b) \\ & + \lambda_{PC} \cdot [p \cdot u_1 + (1-p) \cdot u_0 - d(p) - \underline{u}] \\ & + \lambda_{IC} \cdot [(p-q) \cdot u_1 - (p-q) \cdot u_0 - d(p) + f(q,b)]. \end{aligned}$$

The Kuhn-Tucker conditions are then

$$\begin{aligned} \partial L / \partial u_0 = -(1-p) \cdot h'(u_0) + \lambda_{PC} \cdot (1-p) - \lambda_{IC} \cdot (p-q) \quad & = 0 \\ \partial L / \partial u_1 = -h'(u_1) + \lambda_{PC} \cdot p + \lambda_{IC} \cdot (p-q) \quad & = 0 \\ \lambda_{PC} \cdot [p \cdot u_1 + (1-p) \cdot u_0 - d(p) - \underline{u}] \quad & = 0 \\ \lambda_{IC} \cdot [(p-q) \cdot u_1 - (p-q) \cdot u_0 - d(p) + d(q,b)] \quad & = 0 \\ p \cdot u_1 + (1-p) \cdot u_0 - d(p) - \underline{u} \quad & \geq 0 \\ (p-q) \cdot u_1 - (p-q) \cdot u_0 - d(p) + d(q,b) \quad & \geq 0 \\ \lambda_{PC}, \lambda_{IC} \quad & \geq 0 \end{aligned}$$

3.8.2 Existence of an Optimal Vector (u_0^*, u_1^*)

The problem with the existence of an optimal vector (u_0^*, u_1^*) is that the investor's choice set from which wage contract can be chosen is not bounded. The strategy for this proof will be as follows: We will show that the set of contracts from which the investor can choose wage contracts may be restricted –

without loss of generality – to a closed and bounded set such that the Weierstrass theorem applies.

For any given $b \in B$, let U^{PC} and U_b^{IC} be the set of contracts, that satisfy (PC) and (IC) respectively and denote by U_b the set $U^{PC} \cap U_b^{IC}$.[72] Both sets as well as the intersection between them is non-empty by construction. U^{PC} and U_b^{IC} are closed (all inequalities are weak) and convex, such that the intersection of both sets is closed and convex again. Any contract u from the set $U_{\underline{b}}$ induced by some $\underline{b}$ will also satisfy the constraint set induced by some larger $\bar{b}$, or expressed differently $U_{\underline{b}} \subset U_{\bar{b}}$, with $\bar{b} > \underline{b} \geq 0$.

Expected wage payments for any contract u are given by

$$EW(u) = p \cdot h(u_1) + (1-p) \cdot h(u_0).$$

This function is strictly convex in u_0 and u_1, since the sum of two strictly convex functions will have this property again.[73] $EW(u)$ takes on a minimum on U^{PC} characterized by the contract of $u_0^F = d(p) + \underline{u}$ and $u_1^F = d(p) + \underline{u}$, which is of course the case of full insurance. Now fix some other contract $\tilde{u} \in U_b$ for which $EW(\tilde{u}) > EW(u^F)$ and define

$$Z \equiv \{u \in U_b | EW(u^F) \leq EW(\tilde{u})\}.$$

By construction, Z is closed, bounded and non-empty as the intersection $U_b \cap Z$. Letting the investor choose wage schedules from the set $U_b \cap Z$ rather than from U_b, does not do any harm, since any contract in $U_b \setminus (U_b \cap Z)$ will be associated with higher expected wage cost EW as compared to any contract in $U_b \cap Z$. The objective function and the constraint set induced

[72] Note that (PC) is independent of b, while (IC) does depend on b via the $d(q,b)$.

[73] Remember that $h(\cdot)$ is the inverse function of the manager's utility function, which was assumed to be strictly concave.

through some $b \in \mathrm{B}$ is continuous in u_0 and u_1 and therefore, an optimal wage schedule $\left(u_0^*, u_1^*\right)$ must exist by the Weierstrass theorem. ■

3.8.3 Monotonicity of (u_0^*, u_1^*)

The first two foc's can be rearranged to obtain

$$h'(u_0) = \lambda_{PC} - \lambda_{IC} \cdot \frac{(p-q)}{(1-p)}$$

$$h'(u_1) = \lambda_{PC} - \lambda_{IC} \cdot \frac{(p-q)}{(p)}.$$

Since the function $h(\cdot)$ is monotonically increasing in u and strictly convex, we must have that $u_0 < u_1$ at any $b \in \mathrm{B}$. ■

3.8.4 Uniqueness of (u_0^*, u_1^*) given $b \in \mathrm{B}$

For each $b \in \mathrm{B}$ the investor's problem is well behaved in the sense that she has to maximize a concave function subject to two linear constraints. Then the KT-conditions are necessary and sufficient for an optimal solution. This establishes the uniqueness result. (PC) as well ask (IC) must be binding[74] at the optimal solution from which one can calculate the two wage utility levels $u_0^*(b)$ and $u_1^*(b)$ as stated in the Proposition. ■

3.8.5 Interest Rate Behavior in *D*

Given the bank chooses $b = b^{Min}\left(u_0^*(b), u_1^*(b)\right)$ that is achieving implementation of p in combination with some $\left(u_0^*(b), u_1^*(b)\right)$ it must be the case that we have

$$p \cdot \left[\int_{\underline{x}}^{D\cdot(1+r)} x \cdot f^H(x)dx + D \cdot (1+r) \cdot \int_{D\cdot(1+r)}^{\bar{x}} f^H(x)dx \right]$$

[74] This is a property of the optimal solution if the utility levels u_0 and u_1 can be chosen from an unbounded set. See Kreps [1988, Chapter 16] on this issue.

$$+(1-p)\cdot\left[\int_{\underline{x}}^{D\cdot(1+r)} x\cdot f^L(x)dx + D\cdot(1+r)\cdot\int_{D\cdot(1+r)}^{\bar{x}} f^L(x)dx\right] - d\cdot(1+z) - C(b) = 0,$$

due to the assumed banking competition.

This constitutes an implicit function for the determination of $(1+r)$

$$\Phi(D,(1+r),b) = 0.$$

Note that this function is also dependent on b. Partially deriving Φ with respect to D yields

$$\frac{\partial\Phi}{\partial D} = p\cdot(1+r)\cdot\int_{D\cdot(1+r)}^{\bar{x}} f^H(x)dx + (1-p)\cdot(1+r)\cdot\int_{D\cdot(1+r)}^{\bar{x}} f^L(x)dx - (1+z)$$

which is strictly negative as one can easily see from the zero-profit condition repeated above. Then partially deriving Φ with respect to r brings us to

$$\frac{\partial\Phi}{\partial r} = p\cdot D\cdot(1+r)\cdot\int_{D\cdot(1+r)}^{\bar{x}} f^H(x)dx + (1-p)\cdot D\cdot\int_{D\cdot(1+r)}^{\bar{x}} f^L(x)dx.$$

This expression is strictly positive at any admissible D in $(\underline{x}, D^{Max}(b))$. Using the implicit function theorem we can now state that

$$\frac{dr}{dD} = -\frac{p\cdot(1+r)\cdot\int_{D\cdot(1+r)}^{\bar{x}} f^H(x)dx + (1-p)\cdot(1+r)\cdot\int_{D\cdot(1+r)}^{\bar{x}} f^L(x)dx - (1+d)}{p\cdot D\int_{D\cdot(1+r)}^{\bar{x}} f^H(x)dx + (1-p)\cdot D\cdot\int_{D\cdot(1+r)}^{\bar{x}} f^L(x)dx}.$$

This derivative is positive for any D. Thus $r(D, b)$ is an increasing function in D for fixed b. ■

3.8.6 Existence of an Optimal Debt Level for Implementation of *b*

Given some tupel $\left(u^{*}(b),b\right)$, with $b\in \mathrm{B}$ and $u^{*}(b)$ the associated optimal contract, the bank will voluntarily choose activity *b*, if

$$(p-q)\cdot\left[\int_{\underline{x}}^{D\cdot(1+r(b,D))} x\cdot\left(f^{H}(x)-f^{L}(x)\right)dx+D\cdot(1+r)\cdot\int_{D\cdot(1+r(b,D))}^{\bar{x}}\left(f^{H}(x)-f^{L}(x)\right)dx\right]$$

$$-C(b)\geq 0.$$

r(D, b) is an increasing function in *D* over the range of admissible debt levels in $[0,D^{Max}(b)]$ at that *b*. One can easily verify that the LHS of the bank's incentive constraints is $-C(b)$ at $D=0$. Increasing debt will make the LHS of the last expression less negative. What could go wrong by creating a sufficiently high stake of the bank in the firm, is that $D^{Max}(b)$ prevents the investor from choosing debt high enough to make the LHS non-negative. But since we have assumed that

$$(p-q)\cdot\left[\int_{\underline{x}}^{\bar{x}} x\cdot\left(f^{H}(x)-f^{L}(x)\right)\right]dx-C(b_{N})\geq 0,$$

we can be sure that there are debt levels $D\in[0,D^{Max}(b)]$ for each $b\in \mathrm{B}$, for which the LHS can be made non-negative. ■

Chapter 4

Capital Structure, Financial Signaling and Product Market Competition

4.1 Introduction

Financial economists have long ignored the role of a firm's product market environment in its financial decisions. On the other hand, researchers in Industrial Organization have only recently turned to models in which financial decisions have real effects on a firm's strategic interaction with other firms. Brander and Lewis [1986] have initiated the theoretical literature that postulates a link between the firms financial decisions and its behavior in product markets. Their contribution shows how management can credibly commit to a more aggressive output market strategy by taking on debt. This may lead to an increase in firm profit if other firms do not have access to debt financing.[75] Prior to Brander and Lewis, the overwhelming majority of informational theories of capital structure are located in single-firm environments and/or the theories do not model the firm's strategic interaction with competitors. From this perspective it is not surprising that most of these theories have nothing to say about a link between both decisions.[76]

By now these theories of capital structure have developed into a very active field of research and meanwhile there are numerous contributions which focus

---

[75] See the detailed description of this model in Chapter 1.

[76] There are contributions like Dotan and Ravid [1985] which model the interplay of a firm's financial and real decisions, but this is not done in the context of strategic interaction with other firms.

on the interdependence between financial decision and strategic interaction with other firms. Among those contributions are Fulghieri and Nagarajan [1996], Gertner, Gibbons and Scharfstein [1988], Glazer [1994], Maksimovic [1988], Poitevin [1989, 1990] and Zechner [1996].[77] Very recently there have been empirical studies (e.g. Chevalier [1995], Kovenock and Phillips [1995]) which explicitly test for predicted links between product markets and financial markets. In their general results, these empirical studies are in stark contrast to the early work of Brander and Lewis [1986] with its prediction of a more aggressive product market behavior in response to increased debt financing. As opposed to this theoretical prediction, empirical studies consistently find a weaker product market competition in response to a large increase in debt financing within a certain industry.

The study by Chevalier [1995] deals with the empirical link between firm capital structure and product market competition in the US supermarket industry. This industry has witnessed a large increase in leverage during the 1980s, partly because of the leverage buyout activity during this decade. The supermarket industry is not very concentrated on a national level but highly concentrated in the metropolitan areas considered; four chains account for approximately 58% of grocery store sales in the average statistical area. As a response to a large increase in leverage of a leading firm the number of competitors seems to grow (see Chevalier [1995, 423]). This result is not supported by strong statistical significance, but it does suggest that weaker market competition is not due to a major exit of competitors.

Phillips [1995] investigates four highly concentrated US industries (fiberglass insulation, tractor-trailers, polyethylene and gypsum) in which the leading firm with respect to market share undertook a major increase in financial leverage. Market concentration in the selected industries is enormous. In the fiberglass industry for example the four largest firms account for 75% of industry sales. Phillips analyses quantity and price data for the industries and finds that competition after an increase in financial leverage tends to become weaker in

[77] Some of these theories have been reviewed in Chapter 1.

the sense that industry output is negatively associated with average industry debt ratio, while the product price is positively associated with this variable. As in Chevalier [1995], no firm with a significant market share leaves the market as a result of the change in financial policy although some smaller firms do.

There are theoretical contributions which are able to explain the stylized fact of weaker market competition in response to an increase of average industry debt ratio. Examples are the articles of Bolton and Scharfstein [1990] and Poitevin [1990] both of which have their roots in the literature dealing with predation as represented by Dixit [1980], Milgrom and Roberts [1982] or Saloner [1987]. The theory of capital structure in the tradition of predation explains weaker market competition with the exit of competing firms or the entry deterrence of competitors. However there is no strong evidence in the empirical studies by Chevalier [1995] and Phillips [1995] that the observed stylized facts are due to these two factors. To the contrary, the studies seem to suggest that the stylized facts cannot be attributed to major changes in market structure. In contrast to the above-mentioned articles, the work of Gertner, Gibbons and Scharfstein [1988] and Glazer [1994] is able to explain the stylized facts without relying on arguments from the predation literature.[78]

The aim of this Chapter is to present a model of firm financing which does postulate a link between the firm's financial decisions and its strategic interaction with competitors, but which does not rely on predatory practices as the connecting element between both. With respect to theoretical predictions, our contribution will be close to the work of Gertner, Gibbons and Scharfstein [1988], who show that information revealed in financial markets may affect competition in output markets. As opposed to them, we are much more explicit about firm's product market interaction. As a consequence our model achieves to illuminate the link between financial and product markets to a larger extent than their setting.

We present a signaling model in which N firms compete in a market for a homogeneous product. By means of debt financing firm 1 can communicate

[78] See the review of Glazer's model in Section 1.3.4.

information concerning its privately known marginal cost to its competitors. They will update their beliefs upon observing a financing policy, which will influence their behavior in the upcoming product market interaction. After observing firm 1's financial policy all firms engage in simultaneous product market competition in the Cournot style. The prediction of the model is that high leverage of firm 1 is associated with weaker output market competition in the sense that competing firms reduce their quantities as a response. Debt financing serves as a signaling instrument for the firm which holds private information about its cost structure.

The remainder of this Chapter is structured as follows: Section 2 will first present our model and explain how it fits into the class of signaling games. Section 3 will turn to the analysis of the model and present two types of equilibria that may arise. After a full characterization of equilibria, Section 4 adjusts our framework to an existing refinement criterion and applies this criterion to reduce the number of separating equilibria to a unique equilibrium. In Section 5 this unique equilibrium is studied with regard to its predictions about a linkage of product and financial markets. Finally, Section 6 presents a conclusion and discusses the models compatibility with the empirical studies of Chevalier [1995] and Phillips[1995]. All technical details are relegated to an Appendix.

4.2 The Model

4.2.1 Framework and Timing

There are N $(N \geq 2)$ firms in the model which strategically interact in a market for a homogeneous product. Furthermore, there are two other players in the game, bank and nature, neither of which interact strategically with any other player. All firms and the bank are risk neutral and each firm is run by a perfectly loyal management who strives only for payoff maximization of the firms stakeholders. No moral hazard problem of any kind as described in Jensen and Meckling [1976] prevails. To be more precise, neither the relationship between equityholders and management nor the relationship between equityholders and debtholders is burdened by a conflict of interests. Rather, control is delegated to a management who is maximizing the aggregate payoff to all stakeholders. This assumption helps to avoid the strategic effect of debt as described in Brander and Lewis [1986] that leads to the prediction of more aggressive behavior on output markets as a consequence of debt financing.[79] Imposing the assumption that management is maximizing stakeholders aggregate payoff will furthermore rule out strange product market behavior as we will see further below.

In order to produce, each firm has to install machinery which costs a fixed amount of $K > 0$. Once in place, this machinery enables the firm to produce as much of good x as it likes at a constant marginal cost. The resale value of machines is 0 after the firm has installed them, i.e. investment is sunk once a firm has decided to invest. Firms are symmetric in all but one respect, their marginal cost. Firm 1's marginal cost are either high or low, i.e. $c_1^t, t \in \{H, L\}$ with $0 \leq c_1^L \leq c_1^H$. This cost type is privately known to firm 1. All remaining firms have identical marginal costs of $c > 0$ which is common knowledge to all firms in the economy. Assume furthermore that $c_1^H \leq c$.

Firms 2 to N hold symmetric prior beliefs about the cost structure of firm 1, where these prior beliefs are given by $\left(\mu_0\left(c_1^L\right), \mu_0\left(c_1^H\right)\right)$ with

$$\sum_{t \in T} \mu_0\left(c_1^t\right) = 1.$$

Each firm has enough funds to finance set-up costs without relying on any other financing sources, but in addition to internal financing firm 1 has access to bank credit. As we will see, making this financial source available to all other firms as well does not change our results. The only reason why a firm might want to take on debt in our model is to communicate information about its cost to competitors. Since debt has no strategic effect here and firm n's cost type is common knowledge, firm n cannot gain anything by taking on debt. If one assumes that there are arbitrarily small administrative cost of taking on debt

---

[79] One element of our model is especially adopted to avoid the strategic effect encountered in Brander and Lewis: A stochastic shock to firm profits is introduced an additive way rather than in a multiplicative way as in the literature following Brander and Lewis. We will comment on this issue below.

these firms will strictly prefer not to take on any debt at all. Thus there is no harm in not modelling the financing decisions of competing firms.

If firm 1 goes bankrupt for whatever reason, it suffers bankruptcy cost of $B > 0$. These costs are to capture the forgone future cash flow which could have been generated in (unmodelled) future periods and the cost due to the termination of employment relationships and relationships with suppliers and customers. In general, B comprises the costs to all stakeholders of the firm which is a very broad definition in the sense of Merton [1989, 45] or more generally in the spirit of the stakeholder view.[80] Thus, bankruptcy cost are not as narrowly defined here as they are in Chapter 1.[81] Instead of only containing legal costs and administrative cost as argued by Altman [1984], or reputational cost as put forward by Gilson [1989], they will, for example, include employees' costs to look for a new job.

The timing of events is as follows. At point 1 in time nature chooses firm 1's cost type which is immediately revealed to this firm. For all of what follows we assume that all firms want to invest under common knowledge about either one of firm 1's cost types. Opponents remain ignorant about this parameter but they are aware that nature determines low cost with probability μ_0 and high cost with probability $(1-\mu_0)$, which constitutes their prior beliefs. At point 2 in time firm 1 chooses its debt financing of the project. The banking sector is perfectly competitive and highly developed so that any bank can instantaneously identify a firm 1s cost type if it approaches the bank for credit. Firm 1 chooses debt levels from the interval $[0,K]$, i.e. firm 1 cannot take on more debt than actually needed to finance the project or to put it differently, leverage cannot exceed 100%. Due to a zero profit condition for the banking sector, the bank will for any D demanded by a type $c_1^t, t = \{H, L\}$ charge an interest rate $(1+r_t)$ which just covers its refinancing costs $(1 + z)$. This latter rate is at the same time the riskless rate at which one can deposit money with the bank.

[80] See Keasey, Thompson and Wright [1997, 8] for a brief exposition of the stakeholder approach to the theory of the firm.
[81] See our detailed comments on bankruptcy cost starting in Chapter 1.

Bankruptcy is defined as a state in which current receipts are insufficient to repay outstanding debt obligations. If the bank was involved into the firm's business with some loan $D > 0$ it will become residual claimant of the firm in such a situation. To ensure that the bank cannot satisfy its disappointed claims from any sources but receipts generated assume that the firm has paid out all retained earnings after machines have been installed.

All opponents observe firm 1's financial choice, however none of them can infer at what terms the bank is granting the loan (the knowledge of $(1+r_t)$ essentially reveals firm 1's cost type). Upon observing the financial choice each firm $n, n = 2,..., N$ updates its beliefs about firm 1's cost type. This is done in a symmetric way, meaning that all competing firms are using the same updating rule. The updating leads to posterior beliefs $(\mu(c_1^L|D), \mu(c_1^H|D,))$ with

$$\sum_{t \in T} \mu_n \mu(c_1^t|D) = 1.$$

We will frequently refer to given beliefs as $(\mu, (1-\mu))$ with $0 \leq \mu \leq 1$ with μ as the probability mass put on firm 1 being of low cost and $(1-\mu)$ as the probability mass put on the high cost type.

Before firms make their production decisions at date 4 a random shock occurs at date 3 which affects firm 1's profit from the Cournot interaction in an additive way. This shock is drawn from a uniform distribution with support $[\underline{\varepsilon}, \bar{\varepsilon}]$. The assumption that only firm 1 is suffering from this shock is of course restrictive, however it is only taken to make debt risky. One could easily add firm-specific shocks for all other firms but this would make the model complicated without leading to any further insights. The distribution $f(\varepsilon)$ is common knowledge to all participants of the game. In order to stress the adverse impact of this random shock we assume that the support is some interval of the real line with $\infty < \underline{\varepsilon} < \bar{\varepsilon} \leq 0$. Note that we restrict ourselves to a uniform distribution. This assumption will drastically simplify our analysis of the game as we will see when we turn to the equilibrium analysis of the game.

At point 4 in time firms enter an output stage in which they (simultaneously) interact in a market for a homogeneous product. This interaction takes place in a Cournot style. The inverse demand function is given by

$$P = A - x_1 - x_{-1},$$

where P is the price at which the homogeneous product trades. x_1 is the quantity of good x produced by firm 1 and x_{-1} is shorthand for the quantities produced by all other firms except for firm 1. Assume that $A > 2 \cdot c$. Now firms simultaneously make their production decisions. Firm 1 decides on the prevailing beliefs (induced by its choice of capital structure) and its true type, while firms 2 to N base their quantity decisions on their beliefs only. Note that the interaction in the output stage is not a proper subgame since the opponent firms are ignorant about firm 1's true cost structure when they make a production decision. Following Fudenberg and Tirole [1992, 331] we will refer to the output stage in our game as a "continuation game". At date 5 asymmetric information is resolved and each firm obtains its payoff. Firm 1 incurs bankruptcy cost if it cannot repay its debt.

Denote with π_{1L}^{SI} the profit of a low-cost firm in a Cournot market interaction with symmetric information about firm 1's cost. We assume that $\underline{\varepsilon}$ is sufficiently low (or large in its absolute value) so that firm 1 can go bankrupt even though it has not taken on any debt at all.[82] One can imagine that this shock is some random shock to firm 1's fixed cost, such as an expensive law suit or the like.

It would be more realistic to make the size of the market (i.e. the parameter A in the inverse demand function) random, but this would lead to strategic effects of debt as in Brander and Lewis [1986] which we want to exclude here.[83] We therefore follow Poitevin [1989, 1990] in making this shock additive. Apart

[82] This assumption is only made for technical purposes. It is intended to simplify analysis in the sense that we can avoid complications related to the fact that the firm might not go bankrupt at a given level of debt due to its certain profit. A famous reference which relies on a similar assumption for the same reason is Grossman and Hart [1982].

[83] See the detailed description of their model in the Chapter 1.

from that, our stakeholder perspective will side-step such an effect as well. This perspective will furthermore rule out strange behavior of firm 1 in the Cournot stage due to the fact that the firm is sure to go bankrupt and unable to generate any receipts to equityholders. If the manager makes production decisions in the interest of all stakeholders, he will choose the profit maximizing production level in every case. We will come back to this assumption in the next Section.

The following figure summarizes the timing of this game.

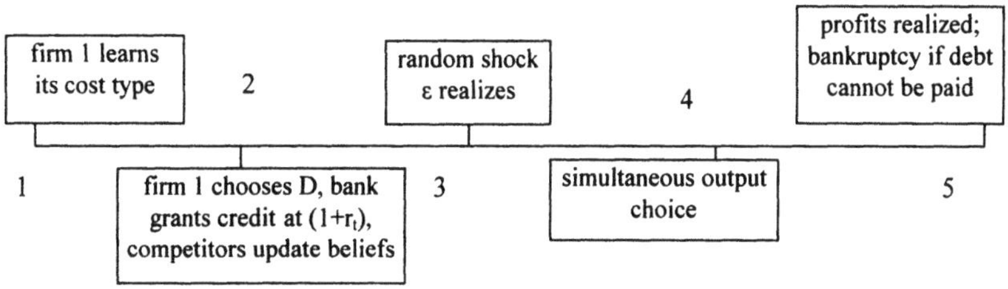

Figure 4.1: Timing of Events.

4.2.2 Firm Behavior in the Continuation Game

It is helpful to discuss the behavior of firms in the output stage before we turn to more general equilibrium considerations. As the model is set up firm 1's quantity decision and the decision of all other firms will not be affected by the random shock. Investment is sunk when it comes to the manager making a production decision. Even though it might already be clear that profit from the Cournot interaction is not sufficient to repay outstanding debt, closing down the firm and selling the machinery does not help to recover any funds for the bank who will be residual claimant. Since management is running the firm in the best interest of all stakeholders it will attempt to recover as much funds for the bank as possible if bankruptcy is indeed unavoidable. That is, the manager of firm 1 will pick the profit maximizing quantity to generate a large dividend payment for the shareholders or to recover as much funds as possible for the bank.

The interaction of firms for given beliefs is a standard Cournot interaction under incomplete information as for example described in Saloner [1987]. It is therefore possible to derive each firm's best response function for given beliefs about cost types $(\mu,(1-\mu))$. This is demonstrated in the Appendix. These functions allow us to calculate optimal quantities, price and profits for exogenous beliefs. Cournot interaction for each type $t \in \{H,L\}$ is well behaved in the sense that quantities, price and profits are strictly positive for any beliefs $(\mu,(1-\mu))$ with $\mu \in [0,1]$.[84]

4.2.3 Interest Rate and Payoff to Firm Stakeholders

Imagine that firm 1 has taken on some debt D at an interest rate of $(1+r_t)$. The financial choice has induced beliefs on the basis of which one can calculate the best response functions and profits in the continuation game. There will then be some critical state $\hat{\varepsilon}$ below which firm 1 is unable to service its debt obligation $D \cdot (1+r_t)$.

Definition 5 For some $D \cdot (1+r_t)$ and induced beliefs $(\mu(D),(1-\mu(D)))$ with $0 \leq \mu(D) \leq 1$ let $\hat{\varepsilon}$ denote the critical state of nature in the interval $[\underline{\varepsilon},\overline{\varepsilon}]$ below which a firm defaults on its debt obligation given optimal play in the continuation game $\left(x_1^*(\mu(D),t),x_{-1}^*(\mu(D))\right)$. This critical state is implicitly defined by

$$\mu_1^t\left(x_1^*(\mu(D),t),x_{-1}^*(\mu(D))\right) - D \cdot (1+r_t) + \hat{\varepsilon} = 0 .$$

As one can see $\hat{\varepsilon}$ will depend on parameters like the debt level and the interest rate but also on beliefs and firm 1's true type. The bank will participate only if

[84] One might wonder who is willing to pay for the variable cost when it is already clear that profit from Cournot interaction is not sufficient to repay outstanding debt. The answer is that the bank itself is willing to provide the necessary funds. This is an example of the case in which it pays to keep the firm as an on-going enterprise rather than to shut it down immediately. If the firm is not in financial distress, the manager can of course borrow against certain future income.

its expected profit from participation is non-negative. Its status is that of a residual claimant in bankrupt states (in which it may even incur losses), while it receives the agreed repayment if current receipts are sufficient to repay debt. If the bank is approached for a debt of D the institution is anticipating the induced beliefs and the optimal play in the output stage. Equipped with this information it can calculate the critical state of nature as a function of the interest rate which in turn can be used to derive $(1+r_t)$ from the zero profit condition

$$\int_{\underline{\varepsilon}}^{\hat{\varepsilon}}\left(\pi_1^t\left(x_1^*(\mu(D),t),x_{-1}^*(\mu(D))\right)+\varepsilon\right)f(\varepsilon)d\varepsilon+D\cdot(1+r_t)\cdot\int_{\hat{\varepsilon}}^{\bar{\varepsilon}}f(\varepsilon)d\varepsilon-D\cdot(1+z)=0\,.$$

Let us now comment on the additivity of the stochastic shock ε to firm profit. It seems more natural to model this shock in terms of the demand parameter A. This would have a neat interpretation: a demand uncertainty of firms with production decision to be taken before this uncertainty is resolved. It turns out that modelling risky profit in that specific way leads to strategic results as described in Brander and Lewis [1986]. The reason for that lies in the effect of debt financing on marginal productivity as described in Subsection 1.3.4 in the first Chapter of this book. The additivity of the stochastic shock is thus a feature which is adopted in order to produce a strategic effect different from the effects described in Brander and Lewis. Of course the interpretation of an additive shock is not as intuitive as the demand uncertainty captured by a stochastic A. In terms of an economic interpretation one could think of an expensive law suit or a tax payment.

One can show that the interest rate $(1+r_H)$ charged for some $D\in[0,D]$ exceeds the interest rate $(1+r_L)$. It is furthermore straightforward to show that $\hat{\varepsilon}_H>\hat{\varepsilon}_L$ at any D and induced beliefs $\mu(D)$. The expected payoff of other stakeholders consists of expected dividends accruing to equityholders minus expected interest payments and expected bankruptcy cost to other stakeholders such as employees. Apart from that one must subtract the opportunity cost of funds invested into the firm. The following expression should be self-explaining:

$$\int_{\hat{\varepsilon}}^{\bar{\varepsilon}} \left(\pi_1^t\left(x_1^*(\mu(D),t), x_{-1}^*(\mu(D))\right) + \varepsilon\right) f(\varepsilon) d\varepsilon$$

$$- D \cdot (1 + r_t) \cdot \int_{\hat{\varepsilon}}^{\bar{\varepsilon}} f(\varepsilon) d\varepsilon - B \cdot \int_{\underline{\varepsilon}}^{\hat{\varepsilon}} f(\varepsilon) d\varepsilon$$

$$- (K - D) \cdot (1 + z).$$

Aggregating both expected payoffs brings us to the expected payoff to all stakeholders of firm 1 which we will refer to as $\Pi_1^t t \in \{H, L\}$. This expression is given by

$$\int_{\underline{\varepsilon}}^{\bar{\varepsilon}} \left(\pi_1^t\left(x_1^*(\mu,t), x_{-1}^*(\mu)\right) + \varepsilon\right) f(\varepsilon) d\varepsilon - B \cdot (1 + r_t) \cdot \int_{\underline{\varepsilon}}^{\hat{\varepsilon}} f(\varepsilon) d\varepsilon - K \cdot (1 + z).$$

Since firms 2 to N do not take on any debt and do not suffer from the random shock, firm n's payoff from optimal play in the output stage is given by

$$\pi_n\left(\bar{x}_1(\mu,t), x_n^*(\mu), x_2^*(\mu), \ldots, x_{n-1}^*(\mu), x_{n+1}^*(\mu), \ldots, x_N^*(\mu)\right),$$

where $\bar{x}_1(\mu,t)$ is shorthand for $\mu \cdot x_1^*(\mu, t = L) + (1 - \mu) \cdot x_1^*(\mu, t = H)$ since, as we have said, firm n cannot tailor its produced quantity to firm 1's true cost but must adjust it to the beliefs held.[85]

4.2.4 The Model in the Class of Signaling Games

Before we start to analyze the model it is first inevitable to explain how the game fits into the class of signaling games. Signaling games are games of incomplete information in the sense that some participants of the game are ignorant about another player's characteristics when making a decision (see Eichberger [1993, 123] or Fudenberg and Tirole [1992, 446] for an exposition). The general structure of a signaling game is that the informed party (the sender)

[85] See the explicit expression for firm n's payoff from Cournot interaction on page 154 in the Appendix.

moves first by taking some action a_1 which is observed by an uninformed party (the receiver). The receiver then responds by taking an action a^R. This response action has an impact on the informed and uninformed players payoff. The game ends with this response.

Our game is different to this basic structure in several respects. Most important, rather than simply expecting a response by opponents, sender and receivers engage in strategic (simultaneous) interaction after the informed party has taken its observed action. Due to the simultaneous interaction one can imagine that the informed party takes an unobserved action a_2 after the observed action a_1 and after the random variable ε has taken on its value. Thus when it comes to opponents to make a decision they are not only uncertain about who player 1 is but also about what he has done in his second move. Since responders are uncertain about what type they are facing strategic interaction after a signal has been sent is not a proper subgame.

In spite of the above-mentioned differences our game has several characteristics which make it similar to generic signaling games and which allow us to study our framework following the analysis of traditional signaling games.[86] A key component of generic signaling games is a monotonic relationship between responders' beliefs, their response and the payoff to the sender. Roughly speaking, if responders are more inclined to think that the sender is of the good type, their responses will be influenced in a direction which is favorable to the informed party in terms of payoff. Our game does have this element of monotonicity. A given shift in beliefs towards low cost will alter best response functions of opponent firms in such a way that the payoff to firm 1 from the Cournot interaction becomes larger.

This leads directly to a second component of generic signaling games, namely the existence of a sorting variable which can serve as an effective signal of the informed players private information. Debt financing is supposed to play this role in our model. We have already seen that a given amount of debt financing

[86] For a formal definition of signaling games see Fudenberg and Tirole [1992, 458] or Mailath [1992, 66].

will (at given beliefs) involve a higher risk of bankruptcy for the high-cost type as compared to the risk incurred by a low-cost type. But this fact is not sufficient to ensure that certain allocations (namely separation of types) can be implemented. For this reason standards signaling games impose a regularity condition on the informed party's payoff.

This condition is called single-crossing property, sorting condition or Spence-Mirrlees condition. It states that the informed players marginal rate of substitution between the costly signal and the uninformed players response shifts in a systematic way when switching from the good to the bad type. Namely, this shift must increase the absolute value of this MRS at any tupel of signal and response. In terms of indifference curves in an (a_1, a^R)-space, this means that the indifference curve at any given point is steeper for the bad type than for the good type. This implies that indifference curves of the two types can only cross once, from which this condition draws one of its names. The interpretation of this condition is as follows. Holding the payoff level constant, it is necessary to compensate the bad type more than the good type (in terms of a favorable shift of a^R) when marginally increasing the signal a_1.[87]

Parallel to standard signaling models, our framework will need some version of this condition to show that certain allocations are implementable. To be more precise, this condition is needed to guarantee that sorting among types is feasible. Again we encounter complications which are related to the fact that there is strategic interaction among the informed party and uninformed parties after debt is taken on. Due to the fact that beliefs induce best-response functions and not best-responses as in traditional signaling games we have to use a more aggregate version of the Spence-Mirrlees condition. The natural adjustment of the single-crossing property to our framework is to argue in a debt-belief space rather than in a signal-response space.

The Appendix lists the properties of this game that allow us to analyze it following the analysis of traditional signaling games. All properties are

[87] See Mas-Collel, Whinston and Green [1995, 453] on the role of this condition in signaling games and in models of asymmetric information in general.

explained and proven where necessary. Some of these properties are not directly necessary to grasp the intuition of the results, however they are fundamental to understand the equilibrium analysis. The reader is thus strongly advised to go through the presentation in the Appendix, before proceeding to the next Section. The equilibrium analysis will rely on graphical tools that heavily draw on the properties presented and proven there. After these remarks on the general structure of the game as compared to generic signaling games we can proceed to analyze the model. Let us first define and characterize different equilibria and then apply a refinement concept to reduce the number of equilibria found.

4.3 Equilibrium Analysis

We are interested in finding so-called Perfect Bayesian Equilibrian pure strategies for this game. In order to do that we first have to define these terms.

4.3.1 Firm Strategies

Turn to firm 1 first. Firm 1 is aware of its cost type when choosing its financial policy but since the decision is made before ε takes on its realization, it must be based on the distribution over this random variable. The choice of capital structure is observable to all remaining firms who symmetrically update their beliefs upon observing *D*. Given that firm 1 has chosen a specific debt level, induced beliefs are common knowledge among all firms. The production decision of firm 1 will only depend on the financial policy via the induced beliefs as we have explained above. Specifically, the realization of ε with its implications for bankruptcy is not of any consequence for this decision. In contrast to firm 1, a firm $n, n = 2,...,N$, can only base its quantity decision on the belief it holds about firm 1's cost structure. In addition to the above-mentioned variables, strategies will depend on exogenous parameters like the number of firms, *N*, marginal costs and the parameter *A* in the inverse demand function. In specifying the strategies we will omit these exogenous parameters for notational convenience. Nature and bank are not involved in any strategic interaction such that we do not have to specify strategies for them.

Definition 6 A pure strategy s_1 for firm 1 is a pair

$$(D(t), x_1(\mu(D), t)),$$

i.e. a debt level $D \in [0, K]$ for each type, plus a quantity $x_1 \in R_0^+$ contingent on the true cost type $t, t \in \{L, H\}$ and chosen debt level that has induced beliefs $\mu(D)$.

Definition 7 A pure strategy s_n for firm $n, n = 2,..., N$, is some quantity

$$x_n(\mu(D)), \quad x_n \in R_0^+$$

for each observed debt level $D \in [0, K]$ inducing beliefs $\mu(D)$.

The set of pure strategy combinations is given by the set S

$$S = s_1 \times s_2 \times ... \times s_N.$$

4.3.2 Perfect Bayesian Equilibria

We are now in a position to define and to characterize two different types of Perfect Bayesian Equilibria in pure strategies. The types of equilibria differ from each other with respect to separation of types. In a separating equilibrium each cost type chooses a different debt level so that opponent firms can identify a firm from its financial policy. In contrast, all types choose the same debt level in a pooling equilibrium with the consequence that firms 2 to N do not have any reason to update their prior beliefs upon observing the financial choice of firm 1. This Section will first define the notion of a Perfect Bayesian Equilibrium (PBE) in its two forms and then turn to their characterization. Since we put the stress on separating equilibria, we will be somewhat more detailed in the description of this equilibrium as compared to pooling equilibria.

Separating Equilibria

A separating equilibrium in this game is given by

i) a debt level for each type $t \in T$

$$D_t^* \neq D_q^* \quad t,q \in T, t \neq q$$

and a belief system

$\mu_n = \mu, n = 2,\ldots,N$ with $\mu : \mu\left(c_1^t \middle| D_t^*\right) = 1, \quad t \in T$

$\hat{\mu}_n = \hat{\mu}, n = 2,\ldots,N$ with $\hat{\mu} : \hat{\mu}\left(c_1^t \middle| \hat{D}_t^*\right), \ \sum_{t \in T} \hat{\mu}\left(c_1^t \middle| \hat{D}\right) = 1$ with $\hat{D} \notin \left\{D_H^*, D_L^*\right\}$,

plus

ii) a quantity decision $x_1^*(\mu(D),t)t \in T$ and $x_n^*(\mu(D))n = 2,\ldots,N$ for each firm,

such that

a) at some chosen debt level D and induced beliefs $\mu(D)$ firm 1's and firm n's, $n = 2,\ldots,N$ quantity decisions satisfy

$$\pi_{1t}^*\left(x_{1t}^*(\mu(D),t); x_{-1}^*(\mu(D))\right)$$
$$\geq \pi_{1t}^*\left(x_{1t}^*(\mu(D),t); x_{-1}^*(\mu(D))\right), x_{1t} \in \mathrm{R}_0^+$$

and

$$\pi_k^*\left(\bar{x}_1^*(\mu(D)); x_n^*(\mu(D)); \left(x_k^*(\mu(D))\right)_{k=2,\ldots,k-1,k+1,\ldots,N}\right)$$
$$\geq \pi_k\left(\bar{x}_1^*(\mu(D)); x_n(\mu(D)); \left(x_k^*(\mu(D))\right)_{k=2,\ldots,k-1,k+1,\ldots,N}\right) \quad x_n \in \mathrm{R}_0^+$$

with $\bar{x}_1^*(\mu(D)) := \mu(D) \cdot x_{1L}^*(\mu(D),L) + (1 - \mu(D)) \cdot x_{1H}^*(\mu(D),H)$

and such that

b) the type revealing optimal debt level D_t^* for each type $t \in T$ is characterized by

$$\int_{\underline{\varepsilon}}^{\bar{\varepsilon}} \left[\pi_{1t}^*\left(x_{1t}^*\left(\mu\left(D_t^*\right),t\right); x_{-1}^*\left(\mu\left(D_t^*\right)\right)\right) + \varepsilon\right] f(\varepsilon) d\varepsilon - B \cdot \int_{\underline{\varepsilon}}^{\hat{\varepsilon}(D_t^*)} f(\varepsilon) d\varepsilon$$

$$\geq \int_{\underline{\varepsilon}}^{\bar{\varepsilon}} \left[\pi_{1t}^{*}\left(x_{1t}^{*}\left(\mu\left(D_t^{*}\right),t\right); x_{-1}^{*}\left(\mu(D)\right)\right)+\varepsilon\right] f(\varepsilon) d\varepsilon - B \cdot \int_{\underline{\varepsilon}}^{\hat{\varepsilon}(D)} f(\varepsilon) d\varepsilon$$

for $D \neq D_t^{*}$ and $D \in [0, K]$, where we will refer to this latter condition as

$$\Pi_{1t}^{*}\left(\mu\left(D_t^{*}\right), D_t^{*}\right) \geq \Pi_{1t}\left(\mu(D), D\right).$$

Since firms 2 to N can identify firm 1 from its choice of financing, there is no asymmetric information concerning firm 1's cost type in equilibrium. After observing some debt level D_t^{*}, the opponent firm n will simply pick a quantity equal to the Nash-equilibrium quantity of that firm in the corresponding Cournot game with symmetric information about the cost structure of firm 1. Imagine type t chooses the debt level, which is meant for type q in equilibrium $t \neq q$. In other words, the information set reached by the choice of type t is on the equilibrium path. Instead of playing its type revealing debt level, firm 1 is imitating type q. Opponents will then produce their profit maximizing quantity in response to a type q. A deviating type t firm will take this into account and adjust its quantity correspondingly.

If a type t should deviate to any out-of-equilibrium debt level, competitors' profit maximizing quantity is driven by the induced out-of-equilibrium beliefs for this situation, $\hat{\mu}$. Again, a deviating firm 1 of type t will take this into account and choose its quantity based on this knowledge. Generally speaking, in separating equilibrium it must not be tempting for a type t to imitate a type q or to deviate to any out-of-equilibrium debt level. We will further dwell on those issues when we proceed to characterize the two types of equilibria. Let us conclude this subsection by again noting that in a separating equilibrium each type chooses a debt level, which fully reveals its cost structure to competitors.

Pooling Equilibria

A pooling equilibrium in this game is given by

i) a choice of debt $D^*(t)=D_P^* \forall t \in T$ with $D_P^* \in [0,K]$ and therefore $\mu_n\left(c_1^t \middle| D_P^*\right)=\mu_0\left(c_1^t\right)$ $t \in T$, for $n=2,\ldots,N$; furthermore out-of-equilibrium beliefs $\hat{\mu}_n=\hat{\mu}, n=2,\ldots,N$ which are determined such that $\sum_{t\in T}\hat{\mu}\left(c_1^t \middle| \hat{D}\right)=1$ for any $\hat{D}\neq D_P^*$ with $\hat{D}\in[0,K]$

plus

ii) a quantity decision $x_{1t}^*(\mu(D),t)t \in T$ and $x_n(\mu(D)), n=2,\ldots,N$, for each firm

such that

a) at some chosen debt level D and induced beliefs $\mu(D)$ firm 1's and firm n's, $n=2,\ldots,N$ quantity decision satisfy

$$\pi_{1t}^*\left(x_{1t}^*(\mu_0,t);x_{-1}^*(\mu_0)\right)$$
$$\geq \pi_{1t}\left(x_{1t}(\mu_0,t);x_{-1}^*(\mu_0)\right), \quad x_{1t}\in \mathrm{R}_0^+$$

and

$$\pi_k^*\left(\bar{x}_1^*(\mu_0);x_n^*(\mu_0);\left(x_k^*(\mu_0)\right)_{k=2,\ldots,k-1,k+1,\ldots,N}\right)$$
$$\geq \pi_k\left(\bar{x}_1^*(\mu_0);x_n(\mu_0);\left(x_k^*(\mu_0)\right)_{k=2,\ldots,k-1,k+1,\ldots,N}\right), \quad x_n\in \mathrm{R}_0^+$$

with $\bar{x}_1^*(\mu_0)=\mu_0\cdot x_{1L}^*(\mu_0,L)+(1-\mu_0)\cdot x_{1H}^*(\mu_0,H)$

and such that

b) the debt level D_P^* is characterized by

$$\int_{\underline{\varepsilon}}^{\bar{\varepsilon}}\left[\pi_{1t}^*\left(x_{1t}^*(\mu_0,t);x_{-1}^*(\mu_0)\right)+\varepsilon\right]f(\varepsilon)d\varepsilon - B\cdot\int_{\underline{\varepsilon}}^{\hat{\varepsilon}\left(D_P^*\right)}f(\varepsilon)d\varepsilon$$

$$\geq \int_{\underline{\varepsilon}}^{\bar{\varepsilon}} \left[\pi_{1t}^{*}\left(x_{1t}^{*}(\mu(D),t); x_{-1}^{*}(\mu(D))\right) + \varepsilon\right] f(\varepsilon) d\varepsilon - B \cdot \int_{\underline{\varepsilon}}^{\hat{\varepsilon}(D)} f(\varepsilon) d\varepsilon$$

for $D \neq D_P^*$ and $D \in [0, K]$, where we again write this latter condition as

$$\Pi_{1t}^{*}\left(\mu_0, D_P^{*}\right) \geq \Pi_{1t}(\mu(D), D).$$

In a pooling equilibrium both types choose the same debt level D_P^*. Since the choice of capital structure does not communicate any information to competitors of firm 1, they will not update their beliefs and stick with their prior beliefs $(\mu_0(1-\mu_0))$ which they held before firm 1 made its financial choice. Their output decision will then be based on these prior beliefs which firm 1 will of course take into account when making its own output decision. In equilibrium it must not be tempting for any of the types to deviate from the equilibrium debt level D_P^*, which is usually assured by sufficiently pessimistic beliefs about the cost structure of such a deviator.

A Further Characterization of Equilibria

This paragraph proceeds in giving a more detailed characterization of equilibrium types. We are especially interested in obtaining more information about the debt levels that are supporting the two Perfect Bayesian Equilibria. Here is where we need the so-called single-crossing or Spence-Mirrlees condition which we have already derived in the Appendix.

Separating Equilibria In order to simplify notation we will, from now on, understand μ as the probability mass that firms 2 to N assign to firm 1 being a low-cost firm. Correspondingly, $(1-\mu)$ is then the probability mass that they assign to c_1^H. In the separating equilibrium all types will be identified by their financial choice and opponents will behave accordingly in the output stage. Upon observing a debt level D_L^* each firm $n, n = 2, \ldots, N$ will produce a quantity which corresponds to its Nash-equilibrium quantity under symmetric information about cost. Parallel to that, D_H^* will induce a behavior of opponents which corresponds to the Nash-equilibrium behavior in a Cournot game with symmetric information. In this situation there is no use for a high-cost firm to engage in debt financing since this will only increase its expected cost of bankruptcy. Such a firm will therefore choose the minimum available debt level $D_H^* = 0$. For this to be an equilibrium it must not be tempting for type c_1^H to imitate its low-cost fellow, i.e. it must be true that

$$\Pi_{1H}^*\left(\mu = 0, D_H^* = 0\right) \geq \Pi_{1H}\left(\mu = 1, D_L^*\right). \tag{4.1}$$

This condition states that it must be sufficiently unattractive (in terms of expected bankruptcy cost) for a high-cost firm to mimic a low-cost firm. In other words this condition constitutes a lower bound on the debt level D_L^*.

On the other hand a c_1^L-firm must find it attractive to reveal its cost structure to opponent firms. By choosing $D_H^* = 0$ rather than D_L^* it can convince competitors to be of high cost. The profit made for a low-cost firm in the type-revealing equilibrium must therefore be at least as great as the profit which this firm could get by falsely communicating to be of high cost, i.e. it must be the case that

$$\Pi_{1L}^*\left(\mu = 1, D_L^*\right) \geq \Pi_{1L}\left(\mu = 0, D_H^* = 0\right). \tag{4.2}$$

This in turn constitutes an upper bound on the equilibrium debt level D_L^* which must not be exceeded in order to make it worthwhile for a low-cost firm to reveal its true cost type.

For construction of possible type-revealing equilibria we will first derive the minimum debt level that can support a separating equilibrium in the sense that the high-cost type does not envy the low-cost type for his allocation. Here is where the modified version of the Spence-Mirrlees condition comes in. This condition allows us to formulate the problem to find this minimum debt in a particularly simple way. To be more precise, we can restrict ourselves to the local incentive condition (4.1) when determining this debt level. If the condition did not hold, the problem would be much more complex.[88] Now, by virtue of

[88] See Salanié [1997, pp. 30] on this issue.

the modified Spence-Mirrlees condition, we can obtain the minimum debt level that can support a separating equilibrium from the following program:

$$\underset{D_L \in [0,K]}{Max} \quad \Pi^*_{1L}(\mu = 1, D_L)$$

s.t.

$$\Pi^*_{1H}\left(\mu = 0, D^*_H = 0\right) \geq \Pi_{1H}(\mu = 1, D_L).$$

One can see from this problem that separation is most cheaply achieved by making the high-cost type indifferent between choosing its type-revealing debt level and misrepresentation. This perspective shows that a type-revealing solution may not exist at all if condition (4.1) cannot be satisfied for some debt level in $[0,K]$. To be more concrete, separation of types is impossible if the induced bankruptcy cost for a high-cost firm at the maximum debt level $D = K$ is too small to deter this type from falsely pretending to be of low-cost. In order to guarantee that type-revealing equilibria exist it must therefore be the case that bankruptcy cost B are not too low. Assume in the following that parameters of the model are such that separation is feasible. To be precise we assume that there is a debt level $D \in [0,K]$ such that

$$\int_{\underline{\varepsilon}}^{\bar{\varepsilon}} \left[\pi^*_{1H}\left(x^*_{1H}(\mu = 0, t = H); x^*_{-1}(\mu = 0)\right) + \varepsilon\right] f(\varepsilon) d\varepsilon - B \cdot \int_{\underline{\varepsilon}}^{\hat{\varepsilon}(D^*_H = 0)} f(\varepsilon) d\varepsilon$$

$$= \int_{\underline{\varepsilon}}^{\bar{\varepsilon}} \left[\pi_{1H}\left(x_{1H}(\mu = 1, t = H); x^*_{-1}(\mu = 1)\right) + \varepsilon\right] f(\varepsilon) d\varepsilon - B \cdot \int_{\underline{\varepsilon}}^{\hat{\varepsilon}(D)} f(\varepsilon) d\varepsilon$$

The latter condition constitutes a necessary condition for the existence of a separating equilibrium.

Definition 8 Denote by $\underline{D}$ the debt level at which the high-cost firm is indifferent between choosing its type-revealing debt level $D^*_H = 0$ and $\underline{D}$ with the consequence of being perceived as a low-cost type. This debt level is implicitly defined by

$$\Pi_{1H}^{*}\left(\mu = 0, D_H^{*} = 0\right) = \Pi_{1H}\left(\mu = 1, \underline{D}\right).$$

What remains to check in order to establish an equilibrium is whether the choices of $D_H^{*} = 0$ and $D_L^{*} = \underline{D}$ are indeed incentive compatible for the two types of firm 1. That is, do these debt levels satisfy our definition of a separating equilibrium in the sense that there is no other debt level to which a firm 1 of type *t* wants to deviate?

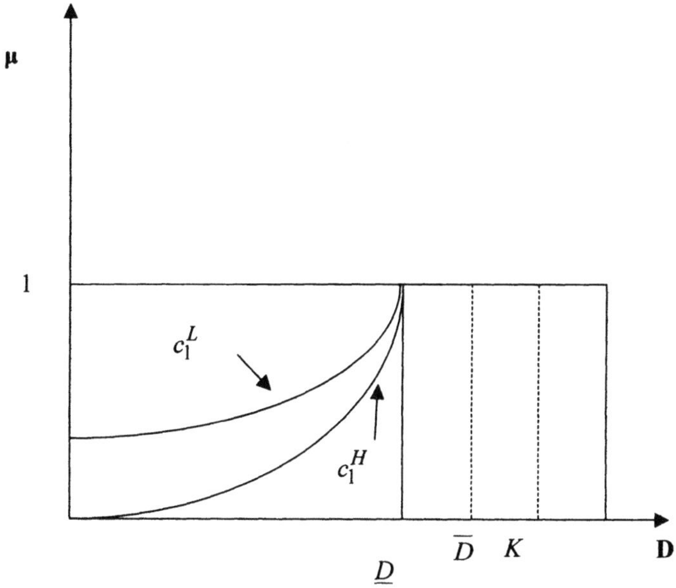

Figure 4.2: Indifference Curves trough ($\underline{D}$, μ=1).

Turn first to incentive compatibility for the low-cost firm. The set-up of the maximization problem from which we derived $\underline{D}$ already makes it clear that such a firm 1 does not want to deviate to any debt level lying above $\underline{D}$ even if it were perceived as a low-cost type by its competitors. We thus have to ask whether it can be worthwhile to deviate to any debt level below $\underline{D}$.

Figure 4.2 depicts the two cost-types' indifference curves through the point $(\underline{D}, \mu = 1)$ in the (D, μ)-space.

From the definition of debt level $\underline{D}$ the high-cost firm's indifference curve must pass through the point $(D = 0, \mu = 0)$. When drawing this figure we can exploit our knowledge about the two cost types' marginal rate of substitution between debt and beliefs held by opponent firms. As we have derived in the Appendix, firm 1's marginal rate of substitution between debt level and beliefs μ evaluated at any point in the (D, μ)-space increases by switching from the low to the high type. By virtue of this modified Spence-Mirrlees condition the indifference curves can only intersect once. Additionally, we know that the high-cost types indifference curve in the point $(\underline{D}, \mu = 1)$ must be steeper than the one of the low-cost type.

In order to determine whether it is worthwhile for the c_1^L-firm to deviate to some debt level below $\underline{D}$, it has to be the case that opponents are inclined to hold beliefs in response to such a deviation which put the deviator on a lower indifference curve than through the point $(\underline{D}, \mu = 1)$. For example, if opponent firms are convinced that any such deviation stems from a high-cost firm (i.e. $\mu = 0$) a type L will not want to deviate. Imposing these beliefs will also guarantee that the high-cost firm does not want to deviate to any debt level in the interval $(0, \underline{D}]$. A deviation to a debt level above $\underline{D}$ is obviously not worthwhile for the c_1^H-firm by the definition of $\underline{D}$.

Generally speaking, beliefs about a deviator must be sufficiently pessimistic to prevent a firm from choosing to defect. Traditionally this is ensured by imposing the most pessimistic out-of-equilibrium beliefs available. The described equilibrium is called Riley equilibrium (after Riley [1979]) or with a more mnemonic term least-cost separating equilibrium. We will henceforth refer to this equilibrium as LCS-equilibrium.

Using condition (4.2) one can furthermore derive the maximum debt level that can support a separating equilibrium.

Definition 9 Given that condition (4.2) can be brought to bind for some $D \in [0, K]$, $\overline{D}$ is implicitly defined as

$$\Pi_{1L}^{*}\left(\mu = 1, \overline{D}\right) = \Pi_{1L}\left(\mu = 0, D_{H}^{*} = 0\right).$$

If there is no $D \in [0, K]$ such that condition (4.2) can be brought to bind, $\overline{D}$ is given by K.

The same argument as was used to establish the least-cost separating equilibrium can now be used to show that any debt level in the interval $[\underline{D}, \overline{D}]$ may be part of a separating equilibrium when out-of-equilibrium beliefs are chosen appropriately. Thus there will be an infinite number of separating equilibria as is typical for traditional signaling games. The nice feature about the least-cost separating equilibrium is that it does not depend on opponent firms' prior beliefs about firm 1's cost structure. It furthermore seems to be the focal equilibrium among the infinite number of equilibria since it entails the lowest expected bankruptcy cost.

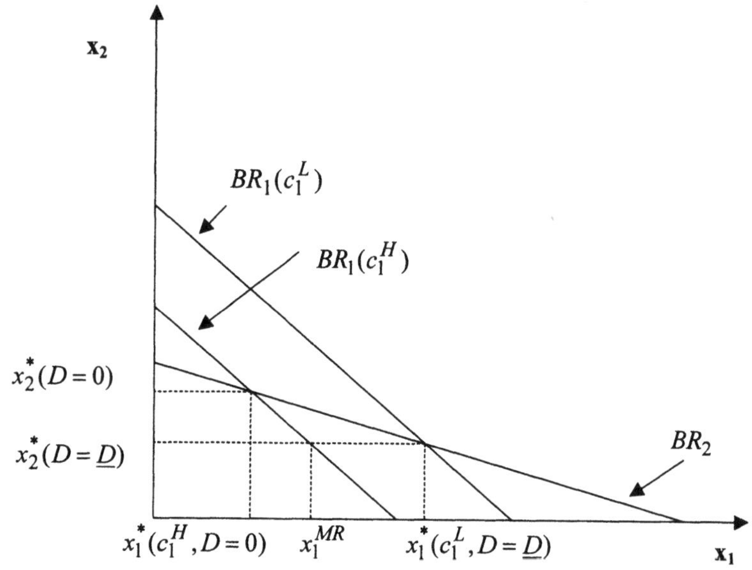

Figure 4.3: Best-Response Functions for N = 2.

One might gain much insight the LCS-equilibrium and separating equilibria in general by considering a scenario with only two firms. Figure 4.3 depicts the best-response functions for this case.

Firm 2 which is uncertain about firm 1's marginal cost will reduce its quantity upon observing the financial policy $D_L^* = \underline{D}$. A misrepresenting firm 1 would produce quantity x_1^{MR} in anticipation of this production and its Cournot profit would be larger that the one it makes when truthfully revealing its type by the appropriate financial policy. However, the expected bankruptcy cost from choosing the same capital structure as the low-cost firm is just sufficient to deter the high-cost type from this financial policy and the corresponding output x_1^{MR}.

Pooling Equilibria For notational convenience let μ be the probability mass assigned to a low-cost firm 1. In a pooling equilibrium both types of firm 1 choose the same level of debt financing D_P^*. After observing a certain capital structure competitors will therefore keep their prior beliefs which were given through $(\mu_0,(1-\mu_0))$. The worst that can happen to a high-cost type is to be perceived as such by its competitors. It can thus "guarantee" itself a payoff characterized by the choice of $D = 0$ and the worst (from the perspective of firm 1) beliefs possible for this signal $\mu = 0$. We can further characterize the equilibrium debt level from the a high-cost firm's incentive condition that must be satisfied in such an equilibrium. For a debt level to be part of a pooling equilibrium it must be the case that the payoff to the high-cost firm is at least as great as if it chose $D = 0$ with the consequence of being perceived as c_1^H, i.e. we must have that

$$\Pi_{1H}^*\left(\mu_0, D_P^*\right) \geq \Pi_{1H}(\mu = 0, D = 0). \tag{4.3}$$

We can be certain that there are pooling equilibria since the two types can always choose to take on no debt at all for which this latter condition is satisfied. Condition (4.3) again defines an upper bound on debt level that can be part of a pooling equilibrium.

Definition 10 Denote by $\overline{D}^P$ the maximum debt level that can support a pooling equilibrium. By use of condition (4.3) $\overline{D}^P$ is implicitly defined by

$$\Pi_{1H}^{*}\left(\mu_0, \overline{D}^P\right) = \Pi_{1H}(\mu = 0, D = 0).^{89}$$

The arguments used to establish a separating equilibrium can be transferred to show that any debt level $[0, \overline{D}^P]$ can support this type of equilibrium. As in the type-revealing case we have to show that the choice of this financial policy is incentive compatibility for both types. In order to make this argument we will again rely on our graphical tool. Figure 4.4 depicts the two types' indifference curves through the point $\left(\overline{D}^P, \mu_0\right)$.

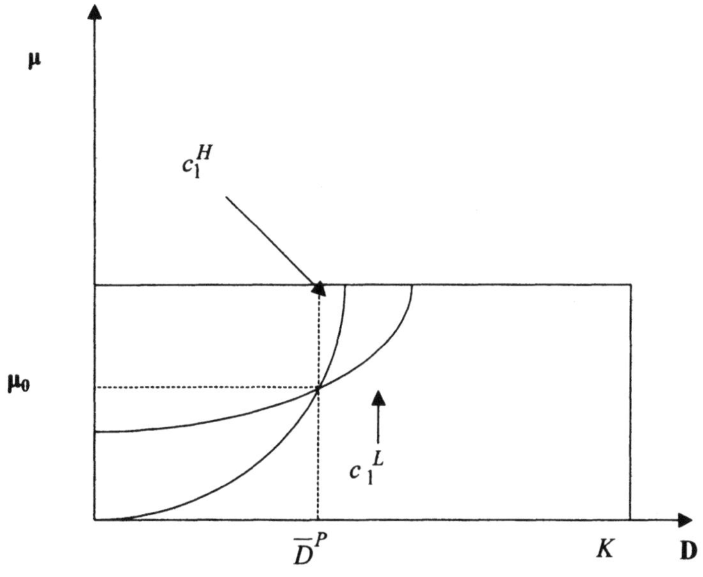

Figure 4.4: Indifference Curves trough ($\overline{D}^P$, μ_0).

The modified version of the Spence-Mirrlees condition assures that the indifference curve of the c_1^H-firm at this point is steeper than the one of its c_1^L counterpart. By construction of $\overline{D}^P$ the high-cost firm's indifference curve must pass through the point $(D = 0, \mu = 0)$. In order to satisfy the definition of a pooling equilibrium it must not be in any type's interest to deviate from the debt

[89] From our assumption which guarantees that there are existing separating equilibria it follows that this condition can indeed be brought to bind for some $D \in [0, K]$.

level $\overline{D}^P$. This can again be guaranteed by assuming sufficiently pessimistic out-of-equilibrium beliefs for any deviation from the equilibrium debt level $\overline{D}^P$. For example, the most pessimistic beliefs $\mu = 0$ in response to $D \neq \overline{D}^P$ with $D \in [0, K]$ will put a deviating firm on a lower indifference curve than the one it reaches in equilibrium and thus it will not find it worthwhile to undertake such a deviation. As we already mentioned any debt levels in the interval $[0, \overline{D}^P]$ can also be part of a pooling equilibrium by the same line of argument. Thus we are again left – as in traditional signaling games – with an infinite number of pooling equilibria.

Different from the least-cost separating equilibrium, pooling equilibria do depend on the prior beliefs $(\mu_0, (1 - \mu_0))$ which opponent firms initially hold about firm 1. The pooling equilibrium without debt financing at all is most efficient in the sense that it does not involve any wasteful expected bankruptcy cost.

4.4 Equilibrium Refinement

4.4.1 On the Multiplicity of Equilibria

The multiplicity of Perfect Bayesian Equilibrium is unpleasant since it does not allow for any predictions concerning firm 1's decision on financial and product markets which is the main topic of this Chapter. This multiplicity of equilibria is typical for traditional signaling games and we should therefore not be surprised to encounter it here.

Game theory has developed tools – so-called refinement criteria – to narrow down the set of possible equilibria in a significant way (see for example Cho and Kreps [1987], Cho and Sobel [1990] or the overview by Kreps and Sobel [1994]). The selection procedure of specific equilibria is often objected to by pointing to the fact that the choice of refinement concept is arbitrary such that the reduction of equilibria is of little help.[90] While we are aware of the problems related to this selection procedure we nevertheless choose to apply a modified

[90] We refer to the work of Kreps [1989] and Kreps and Sobel [1994] for this discussion.

version of a widely accepted refinement criterion, namely the Intuitive Criterion. Because our game is different to traditional signaling games we cannot directly apply this procedure to our framework here. In the following we will confine ourselves to separating equilibria and not deal with the multiplicity of pooling equilibria anymore. We will comment on why we choose to do so below.

The refinement criterion employed here is a modified version of the so-called Intuitive Criterion invented by Cho and Kreps [1987]. It will in fact be able to reduce the number of separating equilibria to a single equilibrium, namely the least-cost separating equilibrium which we have characterized in great detail above. In order to gain a deeper understanding of the employed refinement procedure it is first useful to see what causes the multiplicity of equilibria in standard signaling games and how the Intuitive Criterion is applied there to reduce the number of equilibria.

The way we established a separating equilibrium was to assume appropriate out-of-equilibrium beliefs which made defection from equilibrium unattractive for each type. The general idea of the Intuitive Criterion in traditional signaling games is to impose restrictions on uninformed players' beliefs about firm 1 in response to an observed signal off the equilibrium path. The procedure is to compare a player's equilibrium payoff to the defection payoff it can get by deviation from the prescribed equilibrium strategy. Thereby, defections from equilibrium are interpreted as the reasoned attempt to do better than in equilibrium. If a player of a certain type cannot possibly make himself better off than in equilibrium, opponent firms must not place any probability mass on this type defecting in such a way.

Imagine that for some given candidate of equilibrium there is a defection which isn't to be expected from a bad type since it cannot benefit from choosing this deviation under any beliefs. Furthermore, suppose that this signal is profitable to a good type provided he is correctly identified by uniformed players. Then, according to the Intuitive Criterion, uninformed parties cannot believe that such a deviation comes from a bad type. Instead they should be certain that such a deviation stems from a good type who then indeed wants to undertake this deviation. if such a deviation is existing for some type then a given status quo equilibrium fails the Intuitive Criterion. In this sense the Intuitive Criterion is a negative test. A formal definition of this Criterion can be found in Fudenberg and Tirole [1992, 448] or Kreps and Sobel [1994, 857].

Taking a look at those definitions shows that the Intuitive Criterion cannot be directly transferred to our framework here. The traditional criterion is defined in terms of uninformed players' best-responses upon observing a signal. In our model however, players engage in strategic interaction after financial policy has been chosen and an observed financial structure will induce *best-response functions* as compared to *best-responses* in traditional signaling games.

4.4.2 The Refinement Criterion

In the spirit of the Intuitive Criterion we will now define a refinement criterion called modified Intuitive Criterion (MIC) which is suited to reduce the number of separating equilibria in our game to a unique equilibrium.

Definition 11 Fix a vector of separating equilibrium payoffs Π_1^{*t} $t \in T$ for firm 1 and denote for $\forall D \in [0, K]$

$$J(D) \equiv \left\{ t \in T \middle| \Pi_1^{*t} > \max_{\mu \in [0,1]} \Pi_1^t(\mu, D) \right\}.$$

If for some D there is existing $t' \in T$ such that $\Pi_1^{*t'} < \min_{\mu \in \Omega} \Pi_1^{t'}(\mu, D)$ with

$$\Omega = \begin{cases} [0,1] & for\ J = \emptyset \\ \{0\} & for\ J = \{L\} \\ \{1\} & for\ J = \{H\} \\ \{\mu_0\} & for\ J = \{H, L\} \end{cases}$$

then the separating equilibrium fails MIC.

As the Intuitive Criterion, this modified test seeks to restrict out-of-equilibrium beliefs which opponent firms can hold after observing a certain financial decision of firm 1. Remember that any debt level from the set $[\underline{D},\overline{D}]$ can support a separating equilibrium involving type-revealing financial choices of $D_H^* = 0$ and $D_L^* = D$ with $D \in [\underline{D},\overline{D}]$. In a first step the MIC test fixes an equilibrium payoff associated with any of those equilibria. For each debt level from the set $[0,K]$ step two then defines the set of types J which cannot benefit from adopting this financial policy under any beliefs opponent firms might hold. One can think of four different combinations. The set J is empty if both types can benefit from the deviation as compared to the fixed equilibrium, it contains both types if neither one has an advantage and it may contain either one of the types separately if deviation is only attractive to this specific type.

The set Ω specifies the beliefs that opponent firms are allowed to hold upon observing such a deviation from equilibrium. If J is empty then there is no restriction on the probability mass that opponents might place on either type $(\mu,(1-\mu))$ and μ can be chosen from the interval [0,1]. If, in contrast to that, a high (low) type cannot possibly benefit from a deviation to D under any beliefs while the low (high) type can be better off under certain beliefs, the set *J(D)* contains solely the high (low) type. In this case, opponent firms have to think that the financial policy is adopted by the firm which can profit from this defection and the adopted out-of-equilibrium beliefs must place all the probability mass on this type. Given that such a defection is available for any type, the specified equilibrium fails the MIC test. How this refinement criterion works will perhaps become more obvious when we apply it to our game in the next paragraph.

4.4.3 Reducing the Number of Separating Equilibria

We have chosen to concentrate on separating equilibria and not to deal with pooling equilibria for the following reason. In traditional signaling games with two types only the Intuitive Criterion can finally eliminate all pooling equilibria (see Cho and Kreps [1987, 210]). One crucial prerequisite to obtain this result is that the message space is not bounded from above. If, however, it is bounded from above one has to rely on stronger refinements such as D1 (see Fudenberg and Tirole [1992, 458-9] for a definition of this criterion). Since we have an upper bound on debt levels in our framework MIC is not suited to eliminate pooling equilibria here. Without proof we assure that this stronger refinement can be adjusted to eliminate all pooling equilibria in our setting as well. It would, however, be rather lengthy to go through this procedure which does not seem to be useful given that it would only serve to dispose of pooling equilibria.

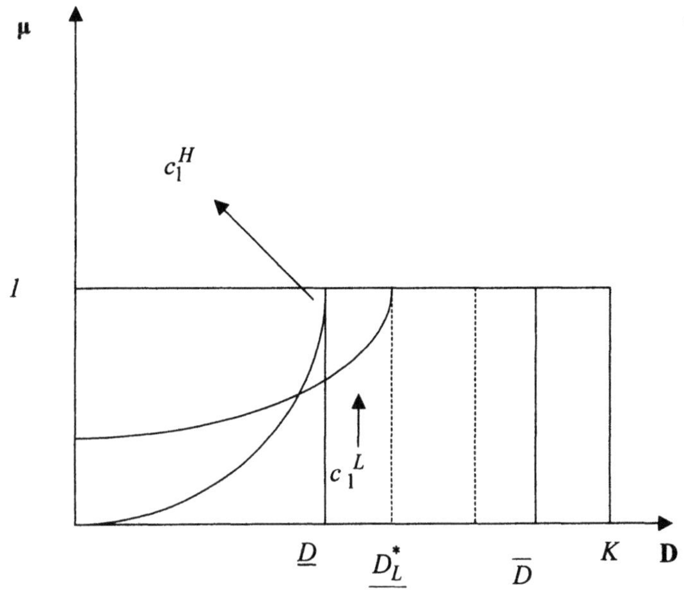

Figure 4.5: LCS-Equilibrium.

After applying the MIC test to separating equilibria in our game it turns out that we can state the following:

Proposition 9 The only separating equilibrium which does not fail the MIC test is the least-cost separating equilibrium involving the type-revealing financial policies $D_H^* = 0$ and $D_L^* = \underline{D}$.

Proof: Fix some separating equilibrium involving the debt levels $D_H^* = 0$ and $D_L^* = D$ with $D \in (\underline{D}, \overline{D}]$. Figure 4.5 depicts the indifference curve through the point $(D_H^* = 0, \mu = 0)$ for the high-cost type and through the point $(D_L^*, \mu = 1)$ for the low-cost type.

By definition of the debt level $\underline{D}$ any financial policy involving a debt level in the interval $(\underline{D}, D_L^*)$ will put the high-cost firm on a lower indifference curve than the one associated with equilibrium payoff. On the other hand, a low-cost firm will be happy to deviate to a debt level in $(\underline{D}, D_L^*)$ if opponents are still identifying it as being of low cost. In terms of our definition the set *J(D)* with $D \in (\underline{D}, D_L^*)$ contains the high-cost type only from which follows that out-of-equilibrium beliefs of firms 2 to *N* are restricted to $\mu = 1$. But this means that the low-cost type has an incentive to defect and thus the given equilibrium does not satisfy the MIC test. This line of argument eliminates all separating equilibria but the least-cost separating equilibrium which completes the proof.

4.5 The Interaction Between Markets

Let us now turn to the theoretical predictions of our model concerning the link between product and financial markets. It is tempting to compare the different situations for the two cost-types within the LCS-equilibrium, but this is not the appropriate comparison to make. The effect of increasing financial leverage on product markets must rather be extracted from comparing the two forms of Perfect Bayesian Equilibria with each other. The LCS-equilibrium strategy combination is given through

$$[\left(\left(D_H^* = 0, x_1^*\left(t = H, D_H^* = 0\right)\right), \left(D_L^* = \underline{D}, x_1^*\left(t = L, D_L^* = \underline{D}\right)\right)\right),$$

$$\left(\left(x_{-1}\left(D_H^* = 0\right)\right), \left(x_{-1}\left(D_L^* = \underline{D}\right)\right)\right)],$$

where the different quantities for given beliefs were calculated in the Appendix, which can now be used to explicitly derive the LCS-quantities.

Upon observing $D_H^* = 0$ a firm n will conclude that it is facing a c_1^H-firm and set $\mu = 0$, while after observing $D_L^* = \underline{D}$, μ will be set to 1. Firm n's optimal quantity in response to each of the debt levels can be calculated by plugging $\mu = 0$ and $\mu = 1$ into expression (4.6). The equilibrium quantity for a low-cost firm 1 can be calculated by plugging $\mu = 1$ into expression (4.4) which gives this type's optimal quantity for any beliefs under low cost. Correspondingly, one must substitute $\mu = 0$ into expression (4.5) to obtain the equilibrium quantity of a firm with high cost.

There is an infinite number of pooling equilibria which may be supported by a debt level D^P in the interval $[0, \overline{D}^P]$. The possible equilibrium strategy combinations are therefore given by

$$[\left(\left(D_H^* = D^P, x_{1H}^*\left(t = H, D^P = 0\right)\right), \left(D_L^* = D^P, x_{1L}^*\left(t = L, D^P\right)\right)\right);$$

$$\left(\left(x_{-1}\left(D^P\right)\right), \left(x_{-1}\left(D^P\right)\right)\right)].$$

Firm 1's optimal quantities for its two types and firm n's quantity are driven by prior beliefs only and remain constant when changing from one pooling equilibrium to another. This fact allows us to compare the product market situation of the two equilibria to each other.

Our model does not allow for comparative statics within an equilibrium. We must therefore use a thought construct to determine the effect of increasing financial leverage on product market interaction. This thought construct will be to imagine one situation (scenario 1) in which the low-cost type cannot communicate its cost structure to competitors and another situation (scenario 2) in which it can. By definitions of debt levels $\underline{D}$ and $\overline{D}^P$ it is the case that $\overline{D}^P < \underline{D}$, such that switching from pooling in scenario 1 to separation in scenario 2 is associated with an increase in financial leverage for firm 1. The following Proposition summarizes the effects which accompany this transition from scenario 1 to scenario 2.

Proposition 10 Firm 1's leverage is positively associated with market price, firm 1's quantity and profit, while it is negatively associated with aggregate quantity and competitors' quantity and profit.

Proof: See Appendix. ■

4.6 Conclusion

The starting point of our contribution has been the uneasiness with former theories explaining softer output-market competition in response to an increase of financial leverage. Models like Bolton and Scharfstein [1990] or Poitevin [1990] postulate predatory practices as the connecting link between financial markets and product markets to explain this empirical observation. However empirical studies like Chevalier [1995] and Phillips [1995] do not provide strong evidence which would support theories of this kind. None of the studies finds support for the hypothesis that increases debt financing are accompanied by a change in market structure or the deterrence of potential competitors.

The main contribution of this Chapter is to show that one can imagine other arguments than predatory practices to explain the stylized facts. Theoretically, financial policy can serve as a signal to competitors about privately known cost of production. This signal can influence competitors beliefs and thereby cause a reduction in their output produced. Our model explains industries' output behavior in response to a large increase in leverage of a firm as the adjustment due to a change in beliefs about the recapitalizing firm's cost structure. This argument is not based on arguments in the tradition of the predation literature and it is indeed able to explain the stylized facts of a reduction in aggregate industry output and the increase in price due to an increase in debt financing.

Although our theory is compatible with these central observation some self-criticism seems to be in place since one can put forward good arguments against our theory as well. As a theoretical point it is certainly problematic to take our model at face value since it does not provide any basis for actual comparative statics in debt. Proposition (10) merely compares different equilibria associated with different levels of debt financing. Apart from that there are two empirical facts which are not compatible with our theoretical predictions. First of all, Chevalier [1995, 418] finds a positive return response for competing firms as well while our model predicts a reduction in competitors' profits. Secondly, Phillips [1995, 1989, table 1] finds that some firms that sharply increased their debt financing have lost market share as opposed to our theoretical prediction according to which market share should rise.

4.7 Appendix

4.7.1 Cournot Interaction for Exogenous Beliefs

Fix opponents' symmetric beliefs upon observing a financial policy $D \in [=, K]$ at $\left(\mu\left(c_1^L|D\right), \mu\left(c_1^H|D\right)\right) = (\mu(1-\mu))$ with $0 \leq \mu \leq 1$. These beliefs are common knowledge among market participants. Firm 1's and firm n's profits from Cournot interaction are then given by

$$\pi_1^t = \left(A - x_1^t - x_{-1}\right) \cdot x_1^t - c_1^t \cdot x_1^t$$

for $t \in \{H, L\}$ and

$$\pi_n = \mu \cdot \left\{ \left(A - x_1^L - x_n - \sum_{j \neq 1, j \neq n} x_j \right) \cdot x_n - c \cdot x_n \right\}$$

$$+ (1-\mu) \cdot \left\{ \left(A - x_1^H - x_n - \sum_{j \neq 1, j \neq n} x_j \right) \cdot x_n - c \cdot x_n \right\}$$

for $n = 2, \ldots, N$, where x_1^L and x_1^H denote firm 1's output when its costs are low and high, respectively.

Deriving the first expression with respect to x_1^t and the second expression with respect to x_n yields

$$\frac{\partial \pi_1^t}{\partial x_1^t} = A - 2 \cdot x_1^t - \sum_{n=2}^{N} x_n - c_1^t$$

for $t \in \{H, L\}$ and

$$\frac{\partial \pi_n}{\partial x_n} = \mu \cdot \left\{ \left(A - x_1^L - 2 \cdot x_n - \sum_{j \neq 1, j \neq n} x_j \right) - c \right\}$$

$$+ (1 - \mu) \cdot \left\{ \left(A - x_1^H - 2 \cdot x_n - \sum_{j \neq 1, j \neq n} x_j \right) - c \right\}$$

for $n = 2, \ldots, N$.

Setting those derivatives equal to zero and imposing symmetric behavior of firms 2 to N allows us to calculate best response functions for all firms, which become

$$x_1^t = \frac{A - c_1^t - (N-1) \cdot x_n}{2} \qquad \text{(BR-t)}$$

for $t \in \{H, L\}$ and

$$x_n = \frac{A - c - \mu \cdot x_1^L - (1 - \mu) \cdot x_1^H}{N} \qquad \text{(BR-n)}$$

for firms 2 to N.

The best response functions of a firm n is the weighted average of best response functions to a low-cost and a high-cost type of firm 1. For further remarks on Cournot competition under asymmetric information about a firm's cost structure see Gibbons [1992, 147] and Saloner [1987, 171]. From the best response functions one can calculate the optimal quantities for any beliefs $(\mu, (1 - \mu))$ with $0 \leq \mu \leq 1$:

$$x_1^*\left(c_1^L\right)=\left(2\cdot A+2\cdot(N-1)\cdot c+\mu\cdot(N-1)\cdot\left(c_1^H-c_1^L\right)\right.$$
$$\left.-2\cdot N\cdot c_1^H\right)/(2\cdot(N+1)) \tag{4.4}$$

and

$$x_1^*\left(c_1^H\right)=\left(2\cdot A+2\cdot(N-1)\cdot c+\mu\cdot(N-1)\cdot\left(c_1^H-c_1^L\right)\right.$$
$$\left.-(N-1)\cdot c_1^H\right)-(N+1)\cdot c_1^L\Big)/(2\cdot(N+1)) \tag{4.5}$$

for each of the two types that firm 1 might be and

$$x_n^*=\frac{A-2\cdot c+c_1^H-\mu\cdot\left(c_1^H-c_1^L\right)}{N+1} \tag{4.6}$$

for firm $n, n=2,\ldots,N$.

The output stage in our game does not constitute a proper subgame which is why we cannot refer to the calculated quantities as Nash-equilibrium quantities. While firm 1 can base its production decision on its true marginal cost firm n cannot do so and must base its production decision on the beliefs about firm 1. This is an important fact which we will have to take into account when we are specifying firm strategies in the game. Our assumptions $A>2\cdot c$ and $c\geq c_1^H>c_1^L\geq 0$ ensure that this Cournot game is – irrespective of the beliefs that might prevail – well-behaved in the sense that all quantities are strictly positive and so are price and profits. The price at which the good is traded in the market will depend on firm 1's true type as firm 1 will adjust its output to this characteristic. It is possible to make the following statement concerning the type contingent prices:

Proposition 11 At any beliefs $\mu\in[0,1]$ the type contingent price $P^L(\mu)$ is smaller than the type contingent price $P^H(\mu)$ with

$$P^L(\mu) = A - x_1^{*L}(\mu) - x_{-1}^*(\mu)$$

and

$$P^H(\mu) = A - x_1^{*H}(\mu) - x_{-1}^*(\mu).$$

Proof: Plugging the optimal quantities into the inverse demand function yields

$$P^L(\mu) = \left(2 \cdot A + 2 \cdot (N-1) \cdot c + \mu \cdot (N-1) \cdot \left(c_1^H - c_1^L\right)\right.$$
$$\left. - (N-1) \cdot c_1^H + (N+1) \cdot c_1^L\right) / (2 \cdot (N+1))$$

and

$$P^H(\mu) = \left(2 \cdot A + 2 \cdot (N-1) \cdot c + \mu \cdot (N-1) \cdot \left(c_1^H - c_1^L\right)\right.$$
$$\left. + 2 \cdot c_1^H\right) / (2 \cdot (N+1))$$

One can immediately verify the claim of Proposition (11) by comparing the two expressions with each other. ■

We do not explicitly state firms' profits but it is straightforward to show that a c_1^L-type's profit is larger for any beliefs of opponents than that of a firm with high cost.

4.7.2 General Properties of the Game

Our model does have a similar structure as traditional signaling games in the sense that firm 1 (the informed party) moves first and opponent firms (the uniformed) follow in making their choices. Furthermore, our game has the following properties which allow us to analyze it following the analysis of traditional signaling games. We refer to Fudenberg and Tirole [1992, 458] or Mailath [1992, pp. 66] for detailed explanations concerning the equivalent properties in standard signaling games.

Property 1: All players' payoffs are differentiable and continuous in choice variables and beliefs.

Property 2: Both types of firm 1 value a reduction in the quantity produced by opponent firms, i.e. if *ceteris paribus* $x_{-1} < x'_{-1}$ then

$$\pi_1^t(\cdot, x_{-1}) > \pi_1^t(\cdot, x'_{-1}) \quad t \in \{H, L\}.$$

This property is obvious. Everything else being equal, a reduction in the quantity produced by opponents will *ceteris paribus* lead to an increase in firm 1's profit from the Cournot interaction.

Property 3: Denote $\mu = \mu(c_1^L | D)$ and correspondingly $(1-\mu) = \mu(c_1^H | D)$ with $0 \leq \mu \leq 1$ and consider $\mu > \mu'$. Given optimal behavior in the continuation game it is true that

$$\pi_1^t\left(x_1^{*t}(\mu), x_{-1}^*(\mu)\right) > \pi_1^t\left(x_1^{*t}(\mu'), x_{-1}^*(\mu')\right) \quad t \in \{H, L\}.$$

Proof: Writing firm 1's profit from Cournot interaction more explicitly as

$$\pi_1^t\left(x_1^{*t}(\mu), x_{-1}^*(\mu)\right) = \left(A - x_1^{*t}(\mu) - x_{-1}^*(\mu) - c_1^t\right) \cdot x_1^{*t}(\mu)$$

and deriving this expression with respect to μ brings us to

$$\frac{\partial \pi_1^t}{\partial \mu} = -\left(\frac{\partial x_1^*}{\partial \mu} + \frac{\partial x_{-1}^*}{\partial \mu}\right) \cdot x_1^{*t}(\mu) + \left(A - x_1^{*t}(\mu) - x_{-1}^*(\mu) - c\right) \cdot \frac{\partial x_1^*}{\partial \mu}.$$

Firm 1 is optimizing with respect to x_1 and thus from the envelope theorem this latter expression reduces to

$$\frac{\partial \pi_1^t}{\partial \mu} = -\frac{\partial x_{-1}^*}{\partial \mu} \cdot x_1^{*t}(\mu) \tag{4.7}$$

As we can see from condition (4.6) and as intuition tells us, the more firm n is inclined to believe that firm 1 is of type c_1^L the more it reduces its quantity. That is, the first term this derivative is negative. By looking at firm 1's optimal quantities for the two types which are given by expressions (4.4) and (4.5), we furthermore verify that firm 1 will expand its quantity in μ. Total Cournot profit must therefore increase in μ for any type, which is what we wanted to prove. ■

Building on Property 3 we can state the following Lemma:

Lemma 1 A low-cost firm will benefit more from a given increase in μ than its high-cost fellow, i.e.

$$\frac{\partial \pi_1^L}{\partial \mu} > \frac{\partial \pi_1^H}{\partial \mu}$$

Proof: This Lemma directly follows from condition (4.7) and the fact that $x_1^{*L}(\mu) > x_1^{*H}(\mu)$ for any μ which one can easily verify by comparing expressions (4.4) and (4.5) with each other. ■

Property 4: Firm 1's overall payoff function satisfies the property according to which the marginal rate of substitution between debt and beliefs is (in absolute value) increasing when switching from c_1^L to c_1^H, i.e.

$$\left| \frac{\partial \Pi^t}{\partial D} \Big/ \frac{\partial \Pi^t}{\partial \mu} \right|$$

is larger for $t = H$ than for $t = L$ at any tupel of debt and beliefs in the (D, μ)-space.

We will refer to this property as the modified version of the Spence-Mirrlees condition for our game. A detailed proof of this property is given in the next Section.

4.7.3 A Modified Version of the Spence-Mirrlees Condition

The Spence-Mirrlees condition in traditional signaling games is required to ensure existence of separating allocations and it is usually stated in terms of signal and response. We cannot transfer this version of the condition to our framework since we have the additional complication of strategic interaction instead of a mere response. We do not know how uninformed parties will respond to a given signal (debt) but we do know how they will (optimally) respond if certain beliefs are given. A natural adjustment of the condition is therefore to state it in terms of signal and beliefs rather than in terms of signal and response.[91] For what follows remember our assumption that ε is uniformly distributed. Since the density function evaluated at different levels of ε appears as an argument in the MRS, there is no hope to obtain any clear-cut result for more general distributions such as the normal distribution.

Proof of Property 4:

Given a certain financial policy and beliefs, firm 1's expected payoff from the project is given by

$$\Pi_1^t = \int_{\underline{\varepsilon}}^{\bar{\varepsilon}} \left(\pi_1^t\left(x_1^*(\mu,t), x_{-1}^*(\mu)\right) + \varepsilon\right) f(\varepsilon) d\varepsilon - B \cdot \int_{\underline{\varepsilon}}^{\hat{\varepsilon}} f(\varepsilon) d\varepsilon - K \cdot (1+z). \tag{4.8}$$

Note that this expression gives a firm's overall expected payoff Π_1^t, (including expected bankruptcy cost), whereas π_1^t denotes a firm's profit from Cournot interaction.

Deriving this payoff with respect to μ and D yields the following expressions

$$\frac{\partial \Pi^t}{\partial \mu} = \pi_\mu^t - B \cdot f(\hat{\varepsilon}) \cdot \frac{d\hat{\varepsilon}}{d\mu}$$

and

$$\frac{\partial \Pi^t}{\partial D} = -B \cdot f(\hat{\varepsilon}) \cdot \frac{d\hat{\varepsilon}}{dD}.$$

Using the implicit function theorem the marginal rate of substitution of firm 1 between debt and beliefs is given by

---

[91] See Mas-Colell, Whinston and Green [1995, pp. 453] or Salanié [1997, pp. 32] on the role of the single-crossing property in traditional signaling games.

$$\frac{\partial \Pi^t}{\partial D} \Big/ \frac{\partial \Pi^t}{\partial \mu} = \frac{\pi^t_\mu - B \cdot f(\hat{\varepsilon}_t) \cdot \dfrac{d\hat{\varepsilon}}{d\mu}}{-B \cdot f(\hat{\varepsilon}_t) \cdot \dfrac{d\hat{\varepsilon}}{dD}}. \tag{4.9}$$

In order to determine how this expression is influenced by a shift from one type to another we first have to obtain more information about the derivatives $d\hat{\varepsilon}/dD$ and $d\hat{\varepsilon}/d\mu$. The critical state of nature below which a firm defaults on its debt obligation is implicitly determined by

$$\pi(x_1(\mu), x_{-1}(\mu)) - D \cdot (1+r) + \hat{\varepsilon} = 0 \tag{4.10}$$

How this state of nature changes as either D or μ are changing can only be determined by taking expression (4.8) into account.

Let us first turn to the derivative $d\hat{\varepsilon}/dD$. Totally differentiating expression (4.8) and (4.10) with respect to D and $\hat{\varepsilon}$ yields

$$(1+r) \cdot \left(\int_{\hat{\varepsilon}}^{\bar{\varepsilon}} f(\varepsilon) d\varepsilon \right) \cdot dD$$

$$+ D \cdot \left(\int_{\hat{\varepsilon}}^{\bar{\varepsilon}} f(\varepsilon) d\varepsilon \right) \cdot (dD + d\hat{\varepsilon}) \cdot \left[\frac{\partial r}{\partial D} + \frac{\partial r}{\partial \hat{\varepsilon}} \right] - (1+z) \cdot dD = 0 \tag{4.11}$$

and

$$-(1+r) \cdot dD - D \cdot (dD + d\hat{\varepsilon}) \cdot \left[\frac{\partial r}{\partial D} + \frac{\partial r}{\partial \hat{\varepsilon}} \right] + \partial \hat{\varepsilon} = 0 \tag{4.12}$$

Solving equation (4.12) for the term in square brackets and substituting this term into equation (4.11) generates

$$\frac{\partial \hat{\varepsilon}}{dD} = \frac{(1+z)}{(1-F(\hat{\varepsilon}))}, \tag{4.13}$$

where $F(\cdot)$ is the corresponding distribution function to the density function $f(\cdot)$. This derivative is strictly positive as one can easily see. Since for some exogenously given tupel of debt and beliefs (D,μ) it must be the case that $\hat{\varepsilon}_H > \hat{\varepsilon}_L$, we furthermore know that this expression will increase when switching from the low to the high type.

Now, turn to the derivative $d\hat{\varepsilon}/d\mu$. Totally differentiating (4.8) and (4.10) with respect to μ and $\hat{\varepsilon}$ brings us to

$$\left(\int_{\underline{\varepsilon}}^{\hat{\varepsilon}} \pi_\mu \cdot f(\varepsilon) d\varepsilon\right) \cdot d\mu + D \cdot \left[\frac{\partial r}{\partial \mu} + \frac{\partial r}{\partial \hat{\varepsilon}}\right] \cdot (d\mu + d\hat{\varepsilon}) \cdot \left(\int_{\hat{\varepsilon}}^{\bar{\varepsilon}} f(\varepsilon) d\varepsilon\right) = 0. \tag{4.14}$$

and

$$\pi_\mu \cdot d\mu - D \cdot \left[\frac{\partial r}{\partial \mu} + \frac{\partial r}{\partial \hat{\varepsilon}}\right] \cdot (d\mu + d\hat{\varepsilon}) + d\hat{\varepsilon} = 0. \tag{4.15}$$

Solving expression (4.15) for the term in square brackets and substituting this term in equation (4.14) yields

$$\frac{\partial \hat{\varepsilon}}{\partial \mu} = -\frac{\pi_\mu}{(1-F(\hat{\varepsilon}))}. \tag{4.16}$$

Since we know from Property 3 of the game that π_μ is positive this latter expression must be negative. However by Lemma (1) it is ambiguous how this derivative will change when shifting from one to another type. It thus seems as if we are unable to determine how the (4.9) changes as we switch from L to H. Fortunately this is not true as we can see below.

Substituting the explicit derivative (4.16) for $\partial\hat{\varepsilon}/\partial\mu$ into expression (4.9) yields

$$\frac{\partial \Pi^t}{\partial D} / \frac{\partial \Pi^t}{\partial \mu} = \frac{1 + B \cdot f(\hat{\varepsilon}_t) \cdot \frac{1}{(1 - F(\hat{\varepsilon}))}}{-\frac{1}{\pi_\mu^t} \cdot B \cdot f(\hat{\varepsilon}_t) \cdot \frac{d\hat{\varepsilon}}{dD}} \tag{4.17}$$

Consider the numerator of this expression first. The random variable is distributed according to a uniform distribution and so the term $f(\hat{\varepsilon}_t)$ will not change in type. Since $\hat{\varepsilon}_H > \hat{\varepsilon}_L$ the last expression and therefore the total numerator must be larger for the high-cost type than for the low-cost type. Now consider the denominator. By Lemma (1) $\pi_\mu^L > \pi_\mu^H$ and therefore $1/\pi_\mu^t$ will be larger for a c_1^H than for c_1^L while the derivative $\partial\hat{\varepsilon}/\partial D$ will exhibit the same property. From this follows that the denominator will decrease (in absolute value) when switching from the low to the high type.

It is important to note that the derivative (4.9) is strictly positive which implies that firms' indifference curves in a (D, μ)-space must be larger for the high-cost type as compared to the MRS of the low-cost firm in the same point then implies that indifference curves can only cross once. This establishes the single-crossing property in our modified framework and allows us to conduct equilibrium analysis parallel to the traditional approach (see Salanié [1997, 30]).■

4.7.4 Proof of Proposition (10)

Proposition (10) entails three different statements: One about quantities, one about the price and a last one about profits. Quantity decisions in the pooling equilibrium are based on the prior belief that firm 1 is of type c_1^L with probability μ_0, where $0 < \mu_0 < 1$. In contrast, a low type is perfectly identified in the LCS-equilibrium such that $\mu = 1$. It is therefore obvious from expression (4.4) that firm 1's quantity in the separation scenario will be larger than in the pooling scenario. The opposite is true for firms 2 to *N*, which one can verify by looking at expression (4.6). This proves the statement about individual quantities.

Let us see how aggregate quantity changes as we jump from μ_0 to $\mu = 1$. When marginally increasing μ firm 1's quantity increases by

$$\frac{(N-1)\cdot\left(c_1^H - c_1^L\right)}{2\cdot(N+1)},$$

while firm n's quantity decreases by

$$\frac{\left(c_1^H - c_1^L\right)}{(N+1)},$$

which in aggregate leads to a decrease in total quantity by

$$\frac{(N-1)\cdot\left(c_1^H - c_1^L\right)}{2\cdot(N+1)}.$$

Thus industry output in the LCS-equilibrium is lower than that observed in any pooling equilibrium. Accordingly, the price in scenario 2 must be higher than the one observed in scenario 1.

The statement concerning firm 1's profit is obvious since its quantity increases while at the same time the market price increases. Explicitly stating a firm n's profit for the beliefs in scenario 1 and scenario 2 directly shows that profits for competitors will unambiguously fall. ■

Chapter 5

Concluding Remarks

On the 30th anniversary of the theorem that bears their names, Modigliani [1988] and Miller [1988] looked back on how this theorem has impacted research on capital structure theory since its publication. Miller [1988, 100] puts their merit in a nutshell by stating that "showing what doesn't matter can also show, by implication, what does". It is this insight from which Informational Economics has started its triumphant advance as the most fruitful approach to the theory of capital structure until the present day. The central topic of this book has been to examine informational theories of capital structure in order to explain a company's financial decision.

The Introduction set the stage for our own contributions in Chapters 2 through 4 by first dwelling on the distinguishing features of debt and equity which might determine a firm's financial decision. The following review of the existing literature was intended to make evident that informational theories of capital structure mainly differ in the emphasized characteristics of the two claims. While the agency approach and some parts of the signaling literature do rather put the stress of the different payout structures of the claims, the corporate control approach emphasizes the difference in voting rights.

We then proceeded to explain the term corporate governance in order to pave the way for Chapters 2 and 3 which adopt an explicit governance view on the choice of capital structure. The goal of this part of the Introduction was to embed the financial decision into the broader framework of different governance devices as executive compensation, takeovers or security class actions. The ensuing presentation of the two financial systems proposed that a company's financial choice might not only be determined by the attributes of debt and equity or various informational frictions alone, but also by institutional circumstances such as the role of banks in the financial system.

We found two main approaches emerging from the literature. According to the first, the firm's choice of financing is able to overcome problems of asymmetric information concerning project characteristics as it might prevail between different parties involved into a firm's business. Early references to this approach are Ross [1977] and Myers and Majluf [1984], but the idea has served as a starting point for other lines of research, notably the financing literature related to corporate control issues and parts of the literature drawing on the theory of Industrial Organization. Jensen and Meckling [1976] are the ancestors of the second central approach, namely the agency approach to the theory of capital structure, which has also created spin-offs like the incomplete contracts approach as represented by Aghion and Bolton [1992] or the modern governance view on the financing of a firm as, for example, represented by Allen [1989] and Blair [1993, 1995].

Chapter 4 sets itself in the tradition of the asymmetric information approach. This Chapter's key contribution lies in supplying an ex-post justification for the empirical studies which identify a connection between financial structure and a company's strategic interaction with competitors. As a stylized fact, one can observe softer product market competition in response to a sharp increase in the leading company's financial leverage within an industry that exhibits a concentrated market structure. In contrast to many contributions, our model does not identify predatory practises as the connecting link between product markets and financial markets. Instead, we are explaining the stylized fact based on a signaling argument which sees capital structure as an instrument to communicate private information about marginal cost to product market competitors.

Chapters 2 and 3 adopt a straight agency perspective on the financing of the firm. The agency approach to the theory of capital structure identifies two key roles for debt financing. First, debt can force management to disgorge funds which it would otherwise invest to the disadvantage of shareholders. This view is put forward in Hart and Moore [1995] and Jensen [1986]. Instead of merely withdrawing funds from management debt can also play a more subtle role as an incentive device. This view on debts is adopted by Grossman and Hart [1982]. If management is afraid of bankruptcy, debt financing can rouse a managerial interest in high profit realizations, i.e. states which do avoid financial distress.

As outlined in Chapter 1, the most prominent objection against agency theories of capital structure is that there is a whole list of competing governance devices that can contribute to safeguard shareholders' wealth. This objection is well grounded and it needs careful argumentation to justify why capital structure should still play such a role. In response to this objection, Chapters 2 and 4 both take a broad governance view of the financing of the firm. More specifically, financing is seen as a mechanism among others that may serve to safeguard shareholders' interest.

Our model in Chapter 2 can partly make up for deficiencies of models that do see a role for capital structure to alleviate moral hazard problems (e.g. Grossman and Hart [1982], Hart and Moore [1995] and Stulz [1990]), but that abstract from executive compensation as a device to realign diverging interests. Rather than analyzing capital structure in isolation, our model recognizes the fact that capital structure competes with incentive pay to perform that task. If a wealth restriction does not allow to punish the manager arbitrarily hard by means of the compensation schedule, debt financing can indeed be an incentive device which may be employed to induce the management to act in shareholders' interest.

In Chapter 3 financing is not seen as a tool to discipline a misbehaving management directly, but rather as a mechanism to put in place the bank's corporate governance activity which is often attributed to this institution in bank-oriented economies. Financing the project partially by means of bank debt creates an interest of this institution in the firm's success. As a response, the bank is eliciting an activity that mitigates the severeness of the prevailing incentive problem between management and investors. To implement the same managerial effort level, incentive pay must be less sharp as the bank's activity gets more intense. What it all boils down to in this model is a trade-off between the bank's corporate governance role and monetary incentives provided to management. Our model is consistent with the empirical observation that executive compensation in a bank-based economies like Japan tends to be less sharp as compared to the US, where banks are not as heavily involved in a firm's business (see Kaplan [1994, 513] concerning this evidence).

Chapters 2 and 3 are similar in dealing with the substitution of managerial remuneration through another governance device, but differ in respect to the menu of governance devices from which shareholders can choose. The role attributed to debt in Chapter 2 does not require special assumptions concerning the financial system as is the case in Chapter 3. There, the firm's financial decision only gains importance through the unique role of banks which they accomplish in excess of the services of a classical intermediary. Whether investors can make use of bank corporate control as a substitute for managerial remuneration will, in the end, hinge on the financial system and the role that banks play therein.

The theoretical results of both Chapters in fact strengthen the view that financing can play a corporate governance role, since financing does not gain its importance by abstracting from alternative mechanisms. Instead, both models provide a theoretical underpinning for the choice between different governance mechanisms for implementation of shareholder interests. In this sense, our work wants to get to the heart of the recent governance debate (see Tirole [1999,1]). While in Chapter 2 the investor chooses incentives for the manager as a mix of monetary incentives and incentives provided by means of debt, the choice between governance mechanisms given in Chapter 3 is between bank activity (induced by the financial decision) on the one side and incentive pay on the other.

The corporate governance literature as represented by Blair [1995] or Shleifer and Vishny [1997] has identified various devices which can help suppliers of funds to safeguard their returns. Among these are the corporate charter, incentive pay, monitoring institutions such as boards or financial institutions and capital structure. Meanwhile there are many studies of different governance systems and financial systems' implication for corporate governance (e.g. see Buckley [1997], Clarke and Bostock [1997], Kim and Hoskisson [1997] and Short and Keasey [1997]). The focus of these studies is on how well the institutions of a specific system are suited to tackle problems of managerial misbehavior. However, literature is surprisingly silent about the relative importance of corporate governance mechanisms within a specific system. By providing a theoretical basis for the decision between alternative governance mechanisms in Chapters 2 and 3, our work aims at contributing to the literature in this respect.

What our work seems to have demonstrated again is that there is no easy answer to the question why firms finance their investment in certain ways. As the economic profession recognized in the early 1970s that tax-based arguments alone could not provide a satisfying theory of capital structure, the recent shift of interest to corporate governance issues furnishes proof that pure informational economics cannot be the whole story either. Persuasive theories of capital structure in the future will therefore have to incorporate theoretical insights from the analysis of financial systems and corporate governance systems.

Bibliography

Adams, Michael [1998], "Cross-Holdings in Germany", Paper presented at the *16th International Seminar on the New Institutional Economics – Corporate Finance and Corporate Control*, Wallerfangen/Saar, Germany.

Aghion, Philippe and Patrick Bolton [1989], "The Financial Structure of the Firm and the Problem of Control", *European Economic Review*, 33, 286-93.

Aghion, Philippe and Patrick Bolton [1992], "An incomplete Contracts Approach to Financial Contracting", *Review of Economic Studies*, 59, 473-94.

Agrawal, Anup and Charles R. Knoeber [1996], "Firm Performance and Mechanisms to Control Agency Problems between Managers and Shareholders", *Journal of Financial and Quantitative Analysis*, 31, 377-97.

Akerlof, George A. [1970], "The Market for Lemons: Qualitative Uncertainty and the Market Mechanism", *Quarterly Journal of Economics*, 84, 488-500.

Allen, Franklin [1989], "The Changing Nature of Debt and Equity", in: R. Kopcke and E.S. Rosengren (eds.), *Are the Distinctions Between Debt and Equity Disappearing?*, Federal Reserve Bank of Boston, Conference Series No. 33, Boston, 12-38.

Altman, Edward [1984], "A Further Empirical Investigation of the Bankruptcy Cost Question", *Journal of Finance*, 39, 1067-89.

Ang, James S.; Jess H. Chua and John J. McConnell [1982], "The Administrative Cost of Corporate Bankruptcy: A Note", *Journal of finance*, 37, 219-26.

Aoki, Masahiko [1990], "Towards an Economic Model of the Japanese Firm", *Journal of Economic Literature*, 38, 1-27.

Aoki, Masahiko [1994], "Monitoring Characteristics of the Main Bank System: An Analytical and Developmental View", in: M. Aoki and H. Pattrick (eds.),

The Japanese Main Bank System: Its Relevance for Developing and Transforming Economies, Oxford University Press, Oxford, 109-41.

Barnea, Amir; Robert A. Haugen and Lemma W. Senbet [1985], *Agency Problems and Financial Contracting*, Prentice-Hall, Englewood Cliffs, New Jersey.

Baums, Theodor [1994], "The German Banking System and its Impact on Corporate Finance and Governance", in: M. Aoki and H. Pattrick (eds.), *The Japanese Main Bank System: Its Relevance for Developing and Transforming Economies*, Oxford University Press, Oxford, 409-49.

Beck, Paul J. and Thomas Zorn [1982], "Managerial Incentives in a Stock Market Economy", *Journal of Finance*, 37, 1151-67.

Bensaid, Bernard and Olivier de Bandt [1996], "Stop-Loss Rules as a Monitoring Device: Theory and Evidence from the Bond Futures Market", Working Paper, mimeo.

Berglöf, Erik [1994], "A Control Theory of Venture Capital Finance", *Journal of Law, Economics and Organization*, 10, 247-67.

Berle, Adolphe and Gardner Means [1932], *The Modern Corporation and Private Property*, McMillan Press, New York.

Blair, Margaret M. [1993], "Financial Restructuring and the Debate About Corporate Governance", in: M.M. Blair (ed.), *The Deal Decade – What Takeovers and Leverage Buyouts Mean for Corporate Governance*, The Brookings Institution, Washington D.C., 1-17.

Blair, Margaret M. and Martha A. Schary [1993], "Industry-Level Indicators of Free Cash Flow", in: M.M. Blair (ed.), *The Deal Decade – What Takeovers and Leverage Buyouts Mean for Corporate Governance*, The Brookings Institution, Washington D.C., 99-147.

Blair, Margaret M. [1995], Ownership and Control – Rethinking Corporate Governance for the Twenty-First Century, The Brookings Institution, Washington D.C.

Bolton, Patrick and David S. Scharfstein [1990], "A Theory of Predation Based on Agency Problems in Financial Contracting", *American Economic Review*, 80, 93-106.

Bradley, Michael; Gregg A. Jarrell and W. Han Kim [1984], "On the Existence of an Optimal Capital Structure: Theory and Evidence", *Journal of Finance*, 39, 857-80.

Brander James A. and Tracy R. Lewis [1986], "Oligopoly and Financial Structure: The Limited Liability Effect", *American Economic Review*, 76, 956-70.

Brander, James and Tracy R. Lewis [1988], "Bankruptcy Cost and the Theory of Oligopoly", *Canadian Journal of Economics*, 21, 221-43.

Brander, James and Barbara J. Spencer [1989], "Moral Hazard and Limited Liability: Implications for the Theory of the Firm", *International Economic Review*, 4, 833-49.

Brealey, Richard A. and Stewart C. Myers [1991], *Principles of Corporate Finance*, Fourth Edition, McGraw Hill, New York.

Brickley, James; Sanjai Bhagat and Ronald Lease [1985], "The Impact of Long-Range Managerial Compensation Plans on Shareholder Wealth", *Journal of Accounting and Economics*, 7, 115-30.

Broecker, Thorsten [1990], "Credit-Worthiness Tests and Interbank Competition", *Econometrica*, 58, 429-52.

Bronars, Stephen G. and Donald R. Deere [1991], "The Threat of Unionization, the Use of Debt and the Preservation of Shareholder Wealth", *Quarterly Journal of Economics*, 106, 231-54.

Buckley, Peter J. [1997], "Cross-Border Governance in Multinational Enterprises", in Keasey, Thompson and Wright (eds.), *Corporate Governance – Economic, Management and Financial Issues*, Oxford University Press, Oxford, 200-11.

Cable, John [1985], "Capital Market Information and Industrial Performance: The Role of West German Banks", *Economic Journal*, 95, 118-32.

Chevalier, Judith [1995], "Capital Structure and Product-Market Competition: Empirical Evidence from the Supermarket Industry", *American Economic Review*, 85, 415-35.

Cho, In-Koo and David M. Kreps [1987], "Signaling Games and Stable Equilibria", *Quarterly Journal of Economics*, 102, 179-221.

Cho, In-Koo and Joel Sobel [1990], "Strategic Stability and Uniqueness in Signaling Games", *Journal of Economic Theory*, 50, 381-413.

Clarke, Thomas and Richard Bostock [1997], "Governance in Germany: The Foundations of Corporate Structure?", in: Keasey, Thompson and Wright (eds.), *Corporate Governance – Economic, Management and Financial Issues*, Oxford University Press, Oxford, 232-51.

Copeland, Thomas E. and J. Fred Weston [1992], *Financial Theory and Corporate Policy*, Third Edition, Addison-Wesley, New York.

Coughlan, Anne T. and Ronald M. Schmidt [1985], "Executive Compensation, Management Turnover and Firm Specific Performance: An Empirical Investigation", *Journal of Accounting and Economics*, 7, 43-66.

Demougin, Dominique and Claude Fluet [1997], "Monitoring Versus Incentives: Substitutes or Complements?", Working Paper Université du Québec à Montréal.

Dewatripont, Mathias and Jean Tirole [1994], "A Theory of Debt and Equity: Diversity of Securities and Manager-Shareholder Congruence", *Quarterly Journal of Economics*, 107, 1027-54.

Dewatripont, Mathias and Jean Tirole [1993], "Efficient Governance Structure: Implications for Banking Regulation", in C. Mayer and X. Vives (eds.), *Capital Markets and Financial Intermediation*, Cambridge University Press, Cambridge.

Diamond, Douglas W. [1984], "Financial Intermediation and Delegated Monitoring", *Review of Economic Studies*, 51, 393-414.

Diamond, Douglas W. [1991], "Monitoring and Reputation: The Choice Between Bank Loans and Directly Placed Debt", *Journal of Political Economy*, 99, 689-721.

Dixit, Avinash [1980], "The Role of Investment in Entry Deterrence", *Economic Journal*, 90, 95-106.

Dotan, Amihud and S. Abraham Ravid [1985], "On the Interaction of Real and Financial Decisions of the Firm under Uncertainty", *Journal of Finance*, 40, 501-17.

Edwards, Jeremy and Klaus Fischer [1994], *Banks, Finance and Investment in Germany*, Cambridge University Press, Cambridge.

Edwards, Jeremy and Marcus Nibel [1998], "Corporate Governance in Germany: The Influence of Banks and Large Equity-Holders", University of Cambridge, mimeo.

Eichberger, Jürgen [1993], *Game Theory for Economists*, Academic Press, San Diego.

Eichberger, Jürgen and Ian Harper [1997], *Financial Economics*, Oxford University Press, Oxford.

Emmons, William R. and Frank A. Schmid [1998], "Universal Banking, Control Rights and Corporate Finance in Germany", Federal Reserve Bank of St. Louis Review 80, 19-42.

Erlei, Mathias and Udo Schmidt-Mohr [1996], "Vermögensspezifizität, Agency-Kosten und Kapitalstruktur", *Zeitschrift für Wirtschafts- und Sozialwissenschaften*, 116, 561-91.

Fama, Eugene F. [1980], "Agency Problems and the Theory of the Firm", *Journal of Political Economy*, 88, 288-307.

Fama, Eugene F. [1985], "What's Different About Banks?", *Journal of Monetary Economics*, 15, 29-39.

Fama, Eugene F. and Michael C. Jensen [1983a], "Separation of Ownership and Control", *Journal of Law and Economics*, 26, 301-25.

Fama, Eugene F. and Michael C. Jensen [1983b], "Agency Problems and Residual Claims", *Journal of Law and Economics*, 26, 327.

Firth, Michael [1995], "The Impact of Institutional Stockholders and Managerial Interests on the Capital Structure of Firms", *Managerial and Decision Economics*, 16, 167-75.

FitzRoy, Felix R. and Kornelius Kraft [1995], "On the Choice of Incentives in Firms", *Journal of Economic Behavior and Organization*, 26, 145-60.

Franks, Julian and Colin Mayer [1995], "Ownership and Control", in: H. Siebert (ed.), *Trends in Business Organization: Do Participation and Cooperation Increase Competitiveness?*, J.C.B. Mohr (Paul Siebeck), Tübingen, 171-95.

Fudenberg, Drew and Jean Tirole [1992], *Game Theory*, MIT Press, Cambridge, Mass.

Fulghieri, P. and S. Nagarajan [1996], "On the Strategic Role of High Leverage in Entry Deterrence", *Journal of Banking and Finance*, 20, 1-23.

Garvey, Gerald T. and Peter L. Swan [1994], "The Economics of Corporate Governance: Beyond the Marshallian Firm", *Journal of Corporate Finance*, 1, 139-74.

Garvey, Gerald T.; Michael S. McCorry and Peter L. Swan [1996], "Stock Market Trading, Price Formation and Optimal Management Compensation: Theory and Evidence", mimeo.

Gale, Douglas and Martin Hellwig [1985], "Incentive-Compatible Debt Contracts: The One-Period Problem", *Review of Economic Studies*, 52, 647-63.

Gertner, Robert; Robert Gibbons and David Scharfstein [1988], "Simultaneous Signalling to the Capital and Product Markets", *RAND Journal of Economics*, 19, 173-90.

Gibbons, Robert [1992], *Game Theory for Applied Economists*, Princeton University Press, Princeton, New Jersey.

Gibbons, Robert [1997], "Incentives and Careers in Organizations", in: D.M. Kreps and K.F. Wallis (eds.), Econometric Society Monographs No. 27, *Advances in Economics and Econometrics: Theory and Applications, Seventh World Congress*, Cambridge University Press, Cambridge, 1-37.

Gilson, Stuart [1989], "Management Turnover and Financial Distress", *Journal of Financial Economics*, 25, 241-62.

Gilson, Stuart [1990], "Bankruptcy, Boards, Banks and Blockholders", *Journal of Financial Economics*, 27, 355-87.

Glazer, Jacob [1994], "The Strategic Effect of Long-Term Debt in Imperfect Competition", *Journal of Economic Theory*, 62, 428-43.

Greiler, Franz X. [1997], "Covered Warrants für Führungskräfte", *Aktienkultur*, 4, 10-12.

Grossman, Sanford J. and Oliver D. Hart [1982], "Corporate Financial Structure and Managerial Incentives", in: J.J. McCall (ed.), *The Economics of Information and Uncertainty*, University of Chicago Press, Chicago, 107-40.

Grossman, Sanford J. and Oliver D. Hart [1983], "An Analysis of the Principal-Agent Problem", *Econometrica*, 51, 7-45.

Grossman, Sanford J. and Oliver D. Hart [1986], "The Costs and Benefits of Ownership: A Theory of Vertical and Lateral Integration", *Journal of Political Economy*, 94, 690-719.

Grossman, Sanford J. and Oliver D. Hart [1988], "One-Share/One-Vote and the Market for Corporate Control", *Journal of Financial Economics*, 20, 175-202.

Harris, Frederick H. [1994], "Asset Specificity, Capital Intensity and Capital Structure: An Empirical Test", *Managerial and Decision Economics*, 15, 563-76.

Harris, Milton and Artur Raviv [1988], "Corporate Governance: Voting Rights and Majority Rules", *Journal of Financial Economics*, 20, 203-35.

Harris, Milton and Artur Raviv [1989], "The Design of Securities", *Journal of Financial Economics*, 24, 255-87.

Harris, Milton and Artur Raviv [1990], "Capital Structure and the Informational Role of Debt", *Journal of Finance*, 45, 321-49.

Harris, Milton and Artur Raviv [1991], "The Theory of Capital Structure", *Journal of Finance*, 46, 297-355.

Harris, Milton and Artur Raviv [1992], "Financial Contracting Theory", in: J.-J. Laffont (ed.), *Advances in Economic Theory, Sixth World Congress*, Econometric Society Monographs No. 21, Cambridge University Press, Cambridge, 64-150.

Harris, Milton and Artur Raviv [1995], "The Role of Games in Security Design", *Review of Financial Studies*, 8, 327-67.

Hart, Oliver D. [1988a], "Capital Structure as a Control Mechanism in Corporations", *Canadian Journal of Economics*, 3, 467-75.

Hart, Oliver D. [1988b], "Incomplete Contracts and the Theory of the firm", *Journal of Law, Economics and Organization*, 4, 119-39.

Hart, Oliver D. [1993], "Theories of Optimal Capital Structure: A Managerial Disrection Perspective", in: M.M. Blair (ed.), *The Deal Decade – What Takeovers and Leverage Buyouts Mean for Corporate Governance*, The Brookings Institution, Washington D.C., 19-53.

Hart, Oliver D. [1995], *Firms, Contracts and Financial Structure*, Clarendon Lectures in Economics, Oxford University Press, Oxford.

Hart, Oliver D. and Bengt Holmström [1987], "The Theory of Contracts", in: T. Bewley (ed.), *Advances in Economic Theory, Fifth World Congress*, Econometric Society Monographs No. 12, Cambridge University Press, Cambridge, 71-155.

Hart, Oliver and John Moore [1994], "A Theory of Debt Based on the Inalienability of Human Capital", *Quarterly Journal of Economics*, 109, 841-79.

Hart, Oliver D. and John Moore [1995], "Debt and Seniority: An Analysis of the Role of Hard Claims in Constraining Management"" *American Economic Review*, 85, 567-85.

Hellwig, Martin [1991], "Banking, Financial Intermediation and Corporate Finance", in: A Giovannini and C. Mayer (eds.), *European Financial Integration*, Cambridge University Press, Cambridge, 35-63.

Herzel, Leo [1987a], "CEOs", entry in J. Eatwell, M. Milgate and P. Newman (eds.), The New Palgrave. A Dictionary of Money and Finance, MacMillan Press, London, 333-35.

Herzel, Leo [1987b], "Corporate Governance", entry in J. Eatwell, M. Milgate and P. Newman (eds.), The New Palgrave: A Dictionary of Economics, MacMillan Press, London, 472-75.

Hillier, Brian [1997], *The Economics of Asymmetric Information*, MacMillan Press, London.

Holmström, Bengt [1979], "Moral Hazard and Observability", *Bell Journal of Economics*, 10, 74-91.

Hoshi, Takeo; Anil Kashyap and David Scharfstein [1990], "Bank Monitoring and Investment: Evidence from the Changing Structure of Japanese Corporate Banking Relationships", in: R. Glenn Hubbard (ed.), *Asymmetric Information Corporate Finance and Investment*, NBER, University of Chicago Press, Chicago.

Hoshi, Takeo; Anil Kashyap and David Scharfstein [1991], "Corporate Structure, Liquidity and Investment: Evidence from Japanese Industrial Groups", *Quarterly Journal of Economics*, 106, 33-60.

Innes, Robert D. [1990], "Limited Liability and Incentive Contracting with Ex-Ante Action Choices", *Journal of Economic Theory*, 52, 45-67.

Israel, Ronen [1991], "Capital Structure and the Market for Corporate Control: The Defensive Role of Debt Financing", *Journal of Finance*, 46, 1391-409.

James, Christopher and Peggy Wier [1988], "Are Bank Loans Different": Some Evidence from the Stock Market", *Journal of Applied Corporate Finance*, 1, 46-54.

Jarrell, Gregg A.; James A. Brickley and Jeffry Netter [1987], "The Market for Corporate Control: The Empirical Evidence Since 1980", *Journal of Economic Perspectives*, 1, 49-68.

Jensen, Michael [1986], "Agency Cost of Free Cash Flow, Corporate Finance and Takeovers", *American Economic Review*, 76, 323-29.

Jensen, Michael and William H. Meckling [1976], "Theory of the Firm: Managerial Behavior, Agency Costs and Ownership Structure", *Journal of Financial Economics*, 3, 305-60.

Jensen, Michael and Kevin J. Murphy [1990], "Performance Pay and Top-Management Incentives", *Journal of Political Economy*, 98, 225-64.

Jewitt, Ian [1988], "Justifying the First-Order Approach to Principal-Agent Problems", *Econometrica*, 56, 1177-90.

John, Teresa A. and Kose John [1993], "Top-Management Compensation and Capital Structure", *Journal of Finance*, 48, 949-74.

Kaplan, Steven N. [1994], "Top Executive Rewards and Firm Performance: A Comparison of Japan and the United States", *Journal of Political Economy*, 102, 510-46.

Keasey, Kevin; Steve Thompson and Mike Wright (eds.) [1997], *Corporate Governance – Economic, Management and Financial Issues*, Oxford University Press, Oxford.

Keasey, Kevin; Steve Thompson and Mike Wright [1997], "The Corporate Governance Problem – Competing Diagnoses and Solutions" in: Keasey, Thompson and Wright (eds.), *Corporate Governance – Economic, Management and Financial Issues*, Oxford University Press, Oxford.

Kim, Hicheon and Robert E. Hoskisson [1997], "Market (United States) Versus Managed (Japanese) Governance", in: Keasey, Thompson and Wright (eds.), *Corporate Governance – Economic, Management and Financial Issues*, Oxford University Press, Oxford, 174-95.

Kovenock, Dan and Gordon Phillips [1995], "Capital Structure and Productmarket Rivalry: How do we Reconcile Theory and Evidence", *American Economic Association Papers and Proceedings*, 85, 403-8.

Kraus, Alan and Robert H. Litzenberger [1973], "A State-Preference Model of Optimal Financial Leverage", *Journal of Finance*, 28, 911-22.

Kreps, David [1989], "Out-of-Equilibrium Beliefs and Out-of-Equilibrium Behaviour", in: F. Hahn (ed.), *The Economics of Missing Markets, Information and Games*, Clarendon Press, Oxford, 7-45.

Kreps, David [1990], *A Course in Microeconomic Theory*, Princeton University Press, Princeton.

Kreps, David and Joel Sobel [1994], "Signaling", in: R.J. Auman and S. Hart (eds.), *Handbook of Game Theory*, Volume 2, Elsevier Science, Amsterdam, 849-67.

Lazear, Edward P. [1995], *Personnel Economics*, MIT Press, Cambridge, Mass.

Leland, Hayne E. and David H. Pyle [1977], "Informational Asymmetries, Financial Structure and Financial Intermediation", *Journal of Finance*, 32, 371-87.

Lewellen, Wilbur; Claudio Loderer; Kenneth Martin and Gerald Blum [1992], "Executive Compensation and the Performance of the Firm", *Managerial and Decision Economics*, 13, 65-74.

MacLeod, W. Bentley [1995], "Incentives in Organizations: An Overview of Some of the Evidence and Theory", in: H. Siebert (ed.), *Trends in Business Organization: Do Participation and Cooperation Increase Competitiveness?*, J.C.B. Mohr (Paul Siebeck), Tübingen, 3-42.

Mailath, George J. [1992], "Signaling Games", in: J. Creedy, J. Borland and J. Eichberger (eds.), *Recent Developments in Game Theory*, Edward Elgar, London, 65-93.

Maksimovic, Vojislav [1988], "Capital Structure in Repeated Oligopolies", *RAND Journal of Economics*, 19, 389-407.

Maksimovic, Vojislav [1995], "Financial Structure and Product Market Competition", in: R. Jarrow, V. Maksimovic and W.T. Ziemba (eds.), *Finance*, Handbooks in Operations Research and Management Science Vol. 9, Elsevier Science, Amsterdam, 887-920.

Mann, Steven V. and Neil W. Sicherman [1991], "The Agency Costs of Free Cash Flow: Acquisition Activity and Equity Issues", *Journal of Business*, 64, 213-27.

Mas-Collel, Andreu; Michael D. Whinston and Jerry R. Green [1995], *Microeconomic Theory*, Oxford University Press, Oxford.

Mayer, Colin [1987], "Corporate Finance", entry in: J. Eatwell, M. Milgate and P. Newman (eds.), The New Palgrave: A Dictionary of Economics, MacMillan Press, London 462-72.

Mayer, Colin [1988], "New Issues in Corporate Finance", *European Economic Review*, 32, 1167-1189.

Mayer, Colin [1990], "Financial Systems, Corporate Finance and Economic Development", in: R. Glenn Hubbard (ed.), *Asymmetric Information, Corporate Finance and Investment*, NBER, University of Chicago Press, 307-32.

Mayer, Colin [1998], "Financial Systems and Corporate Governance: A Review of International Evidence", *Journal of Institutional and Theoretical Economics*, 154, 144-65.

Merton, Robert C. [1989], "Discussion" in: R. Kopcke and E.S. Rosengren (eds.), *Are the Distinctions Between Debt and Equity Disappearing?*, Federal Reserve Bank of Boston, Conference Series No. 33, Boston, 44-48.

Milgrom, Paul and John Roberts [1982], "Limit Pricing and Entry under Incomplete Information: An Equilibrium Analysis", *Econometrica*, 50, 443-60.

Milgrom, Paul and John Roberts [1992], *Economics, Organization and Management*, Prentice-Hall, Englewood Cliffs, New Jersey.

Miller, Merton H. [1988], "The Modigliani-Miller Propositons After Thirty Years", *Journal of Economic Perspectives*, 2, 99-120.

Modigliani, Franco [1988], "MM-Past, Present, Future", *Journal of Economic Perspectives*, 2, 149-58.

Modigliani, Franco and Merton Miller [1958], "The Cost of Capital, Corporation Finance and the Theory of Investment", *American Economic Review*, 48, 261-97.

Murphy, Kevin J. [1985], "Corporate Performance and Managerial Remuneration", *Journal of Accounting and Economics*, 7, 11-42.

Myers, Stewart C. and Nicholas S. Majluf [1984], "Corporate Financing and Investment Decisions, When Firms Have Information That Investors do not Have", *Journal of Financial Economics*, 13, 187-221.

Myers, Stewart C. [1984], "The Capital Structure Puzzle", *Journal of Finance*, 39, 5ö75-92.

Myers, Stewart C. [1989], "Still Searching for the Optimal Capital Structure" in: R. Kopcke and E.S. Rosengren (eds.), *Are the Distinctions Between Debt and Equity Disappearing?*, Federal Reserve Bank of Boston, Conference Series No. 33, Boston, 80-95.

Pagano, Marco and Ailsa Röell [1998], "The Choice of Stock Ownership Structure: Agency Costs, Monitoring and the Decision to go Public", *Quarterly Journal of Economics*, 113, 187-225.

Perotti, Enrico C. and Kathryn E. Spier [1993], "Capital Structure as a Bargaining Tool: The Role of Leverage in Contract Renegotiation", *American Economic Review*, 83, 1131-41.

Phillips, Gordon M. [1995], "Increased Debt and Industry Product Markets: An Empirical Analysis", *Journal of Financial Economics*, 37, 189-238.

Poitevin, Michael [1989], "Financial Signalling and the 'Deep-Pocket' Argument", *RAND Journal of Economics*, 20, 26-40.

Poitevin, Michael [1990], "Strategic Financial Signalling", *International Journal of Industrial Organization*, 8, 499-518.

Riley, John G. [1979], "Informational Equilibrium", *Econometrica*, 47, 331-59.

Ross, Stephen A. [1977], "The Determination of Financial Structure: The Incentive-Signalling Approach", *Bell Journal of Economics*, 8, 23-40.

Salanié, Bernard [1997], *The Economics of Contracts – A Primer*, The MIT Press, Cambridge, Mass.

Saloner, Garth [1987], "Predation, Mergers and Incomplete Information", *RAND Journal of Economics*, 18, 165-186.

Sappington, David [1983], "Limited Liability Contracts Between Principal and Agent", *Journal of Economic Theory*, 29, 1-21.

Schmidt, Klaus [1997], "Managerial Incentives and Product Market Competition", *Review of Economic Studies*, 64, 191-213.

Sheard, Paul [1989], "The Main Bank System and Corporate Monitoring and Control in Japan", *Journal of Economic Behavior and Organization*, 11, 399-422.

Shleifer, Andrei and Robert W. Vishny [1997], "A Survey of Corporate Governance", *Journal of Finance*, 52, 737-83.

Short, Helen and Kevin Keasey [1997], "Institutional Shareholders and Corporate Governance in the United Kingdom", in: Keasey, Thompson and Wright (eds.), *Corporate Governance – Economic, Management and Financial Issues*, Oxford University Press, Oxford, 18-35.

Shy, Oz [1995], *Industrial Organization – Theory and Applications*, The MIT Press, Cambridge, Mass.

Spence, Michael [1973], "Job Market Signalling", *Quarterly Journal of Economics*, 87, 355-74.

Spence, Michael [1985], "Capital Structure and the Corporation's Product Market Environment", in: B.M. Friedman (ed.), *Corporate Capital Structure in the United States*, The University of Chicago Press, Chicago, 353-82.

Spiegel, Yossef and Daniel F. Spulber [1997], "Capital Structure With Countervailing Incentives", *RAND Journal of Economics*, 28, 1-24.

Stiglitz, Joseph E. [1969], "A Re-Examination of the Modigliani-Miller Theorem", *American Economic Review*, 59, 784-93.

Stiglitz, Joseph and Andrew Weiss [1981], "Credit Rationing in Markets with Imperfect Information", *American Economic Review*, 71, 393-410.

Strahan, Philip E. [1998], "Securities Class Actions, Corporate Governance and Managerial Agency Problems", Federal Reserve Bank of New York, mimeo.

Stulz, Rene [1990], "Managerial Discretion and Optimal Financing Policies", *Journal of Financial Economics*, 26, 3-27.

Tirole, Jean [1988], *The Theory of Industrial Organization*, The MIT Press, Cambridge, Mass.

Tirole, Jean [1995], "Incomplete Contracts: Where do we Stand?", Walras-Bowley Lecture delivered at the 1994 North American Summer Meeting of the Econometric Society in Québec City.

Tirole, Jean [1999], "Corporate Governance", Presidential Address, Econometric Society Meeting 1998, Berlin.

Varian, Hal [1990], "Monitoring Agents with Other Agents", *Journal of Institutional and Theoretical Economics*, 146, 153-74.

Warner, Jerold B. [1977], "Bankruptcy Cost: Some Evidence", *Journal of Finance*, 32, 337-47.

Williamson, Oliver E. [1988], “Corporate Finance and Corporate Governance”, *Journal of Finance*, 43, 567-91.

Zechner, Josef [1996], “Financial Market-Product Market Interactions in Industry Equilibrium: Implications for Information Acquisition Decisions”, *European Economic Review*, 40, 883-96.

Zender, Jaime F. [1991], “Optimal Financial Instruments”, *Journal of Finance*, 46, 1645-63.

Zwiebel, Jeffrey [1995], “Block Investment and Partial Benefits of Corporate Control”, *Review of Economic Studies*, 62, 161-85.

Entwicklung und Finanzierung
Development and Finance

Herausgegeben von / Edited by
Reinhard H. Schmidt
Claus-Peter Zeitinger

Bd./Vol. 1 Heike Proff: Auswirkungen der Politik der internationalen Finanzinstitutionen (IWF und Weltbank) auf importintensive und exportorientierte Unternehmen in Ghana. 1994.

Bd./Vol. 2 Martin Holtmann / Rochus Mommartz: Technical Guide for Analyzing the Efficiency of Credit-Granting / Non-Governmental Organizations (NGOs). 1996.

Band 1 + 2 sind im Verlag für Entwicklungspolitik Breitenbach GmbH, Saarbrücken, erschienen und auch von dort zu beziehen.
Vol. 1 + 2 have already been published by Verlag für Entwicklungspolitik, Breitenbach GmbH, Saarbrücken, and are obtainable through the publishers.

Entwicklung und Finanzierung
Development and Finance

Herausgegeben von / Edited by
Manfred Nitsch, Reinhard H. Schmidt und Claus-Peter Zeitinger

Bd./Vol. 3 Ilonka Rühle: Why Banks? Microeconomic Foundations of Financial Intermediaries. 1997.

Bd./Vol. 4 Manfred Kiefer: Die Rentenreform in Peru. Auswirkungen auf soziale Sicherung, Finanzmärkte und Staatsfinanzen. 1998.

Bd./Vol. 5 Modibo Khane Camara: Die Finanzsektorreform in Afrika. Das Beispiel der Franc-Zone. 1998.

Bd./Vol. 6 Andreas Hackethal: Banken, Unternehmensfinanzierung und Finanzsysteme. 2000.

Bd./Vol. 7 Silvio Andrae / Kathrin Pingel: Tropical Finance. Von den (Un-)Möglichkeiten eines ländlichen Finanzsystems im brasilianischen Amazonien. 2001.

Bd./Vol. 8 Marcel Gounot: The Efficiency of Multi-Tier Savings and Credit Cooperatives in Developing Countries. A Study Based on Empirical Research in West Africa. 2001.

Bd/Vol. 9 Christian M. Pfeil: Capital Structure, Managerial Incentives and Corporate Governance. 2002.

For the avoidance of doubt, input of the whole or any part of this publication into any generative artificial intelligence model, chatbot, program, software or technology is expressly prohibited without the prior written consent of the publisher.